# SUPPLY & L

# TRADING

# How To Master
# The Trading Zones

*Frank Miller*

# TABLE OF CONTENTS

# INTRODUCTION

Most traders will agree with me that the financial markets are full of risks. Those risks come from unpredictable price movements in the market, the big temptations to jump on unclear trade set-ups, the psychological and managerial obstacles that beat traders most of the time, and much, much more.

To minimize the risks and maximize the winning potentials in the market, we all need to stack the odds in our favor. In other books, I emphasize on the need for trading based on at least one confirmation signal. I call them "chart phenomena" as they appear on the chart constantly.

This book is different. It still mentions some visual signals on the chart, but the main building block stems from two key microeconomic concepts: *supply and demand*. By discovering how supply and demand can affect market orders, we are talking about the backbone that drives any market operations, not just financial markets.

Trading based on the correlation between supply and demand, we follow the footprints of the big players in the financial markets. You'll get an idea of why some traditional market signals don't work as you expect, and why the same market zone may generate very different winning potentials regardless of other trade confirmation signals. The utmost goal in this book is to increase your winning trade probability – a concept that I don't focus on too much in other books.

One of the most interesting parts of this book is tons of trading examples and illustrations that make your learning process easier and more exciting than ever. You will be mind-blowing about how easy but effective all the theories and strategies are without having to rely on many technical indicators. The scoring system, which uses a quantitative measurement, will be one powerful security shield that helps you to confidently say "no" to a *seemingly good opportunity* when necessary. Also, the book will present 7 powerful different trading strategies based on supply and demand, and this is probably the first time I've ever accumulated such a large number of strategies in a book.

With a clear, concise, and straightforward way of presenting all information in this book, you will have all you need in trading with supply and demand, whether you choose to be a day trader, swing trader, or position trader.

Having been in the financial market for over 20 years, I'm an advocate of backbone elements in trading and investing, and this pings a eureka moment in my mind in writing a book about supply and demand in trading. I want to show people how important it is in following the steps of the big players in the market. This is what we often refer to as "stack the odds in our favor" in trading.

Once you have mastered all the techniques presented in this book, you will be confident in identifying a high probability trading zone as well as entry, exit, and stop prices. You can even look back at your losing trades in the past and easily explain the reason behind the loss.

From my viewpoint, the book will be most suitable for someone who has certain experience in trading or investing. As I said, you may explain the reason for your previous failed trades, and this can only be done with a certain amount of trading experience. Yet, a newbie can still benefit from this book by incorporating supply and demand theories in their core trading system. In other words, sooner or later, you will be beneficial from the concepts I present in the book.

Before we dive into the main part of the book, let's take a look at some of my thoughts before, during, and after writing this book.

1. Treat it as a friend of yours·

As always, I hope you can treat the book not only as a learning material but also as a friend of yours. To me, conveying all information, strategies, and thoughts into a book effectively is never a quick and easy task. There is the editor, formatter, and designer who contributed to the completion of a good book. I hope you will learn something useful in this edition, and treat it as a friend which can help you pinpoint good opportunities in the financial markets and prevent you from taking unnecessary risks.

2. No success guarantee

Although I truly believe in the effectiveness of all trading strategies presented in *Supply and Demand Trading,* I cannot make sure you will make instant profits after reading the book. As I said at the beginning of the book, financial trading is full of risks, and success in trading entails constructive actions repeated again and again. Reading is just the first part of the process where you obtain the necessary information. The next (more) important part is taking consistent actions without losing your enthusiasm and belief.

The degree of profitability in trading varies among traders. Ten traders applying the same best trading strategy in the world will produce 10 different results. Trading has a lot more to do with psychology preparation and risk management. Your success in trading main lies in *how **you apply*** what is taught in this material. **You** are the only person who can determine your success.

3.   This may not be ALL YOU NEED

As you may already know, the trading metaverse includes many trading angles and each of them may give you a different trade idea and method.

Although I believe supply and demand can be a perfect preparation in trading, learning from other sources and books will never be redundant. In the book, I refer to some other books that I believe will be a perfect supplement to your trading arsenal.

Now that we've had enough greetings and gotten to know each other better, let's get started with the main part of the book.

# Chapter 1: Traditional Support & Resistance

Before learning about supply and demand, let's discover two seemingly similar concepts: Support and resistance. If you read any other book of mine, trading with support/resistance levels has always been my favorite technique. In this chapter, we will go briefly about how support and resistance levels play an important role in my trading analysis. Later in the book, you will see how supply/demand not only shares some similarities with support/resistance but also plays as a perfect upgrade in identifying tradable zones.

## Support and Resistance Levels

Support is a price zone where the downtrend tends to pause due to greater buying interest. When the price of an asset drops, it becomes cheaper in buyers' eyes, thus motivating them to make more buy orders and forming a support level. Resistance is just the opposite where the uptrend is expected to pause or at least there are some reactions around it. This is where prices are impressive to sellers' point of view and more selling orders are placed, forming a resistance level.

Once the price reaches (key) support or resistance, traders often look for either an entry or exit point. The main underlying reason for this is two common reactions of the price on those levels: it will either bounce back or violate the level. Whether the price breaks through the level or is anchored by the level, traders can bet on the next move of the market. If they're wrong, the trade can be closed at a small loss (stop-loss is hit), otherwise, they may enjoy a considerable profit.

In this example, suppose Mark is holding Gold from September 2018 to April 2019 with an expectation for the price to go higher. Mark notices that the price was constantly having difficulties in closing above the $1,354 level several times during the period. There was one time it successfully broke above the price level, but it retraced back down the level right afterward. In this case, we call the $1,354 level the resistance level, just like a ceiling.

In this example, the $30,000 price level acts as a floor to prevent the price to break below. In other words, this is a good price in buyers' eyes and they are willing to buy the security at this price level, pushing the price back up whenever it tested the zone. In this case, the $30,000 price level is a support level.

Support/resistance not only forms as manually drawn horizontal lines on the chart. Other common types of support/resistance include Fibonacci levels, trend lines, and moving averages. Let's take a look at how these levels can perform as support/resistance on the chart.

## Fibonacci

Fibonacci retracement tool is a technical indicator that identifies potential barriers in the pullback of the price. This tool can seem complicated at first, but traders can gradually make use of it through practice. With Fibonacci, identifying potential pullback levels doesn't rely on any previous levels. Instead, the plotting of support/resistance is mainly based on a magic

9

numerical sequence. The five most popular levels of support/resistance is 23.6%, 38.2%, 50%, 61.8% and 78.6% levels. Take a look at the example below for an illustration:

## Trend lines

The two types of popular support/resistance above are static levels. However, the price of the financial assets may also trend upward or downward (which is what all traders often look for), hence it is common to see these price barriers change over time. This is why trend lines are an important part of support/resistance in trading.

For example, when the market is in an uptrend, resistance may form as a result of profit-taking among buyers. The profit-taking process results in a pullback, or a drop-off toward the trend line, forming a short-term high during the uptrend.

Notice how the ascending trend line props up the Apple price from October 2020 to July 2021

On the other hand, when the price drop, traders may look for a series of lower highs and connect these highs to form a descending trend line. When the price approaches the trend line, traders may consider entering a short position because this is where the price tends to continue in the overall direction in the past.

One consensus among most traders is that the more time the price fails to break through support/resistance levels, the stronger the support/resistance is. Trading supply and demand is quite different in this manner. Later in this book, we'll learn more about this using the market strength analysis.

## Moving Average

Moving average is an indicator that is used by most traders, whether they advocate technical indicators or not. These traders use this indicator to predict short-term price movement and identify a reliable level of support/resistance. As you can see from the chart below, a moving average is a moving line that serves to smooth out past price data while offering ideal entry points both in an uptrend and a downtrend. Notice how the line acts as support during an uptrend and resistance in a downtrend. The price was constantly bouncing back each time it touches or nearly touches the moving average line.

Keep in mind that the use of moving average is not limited to identifying support/resistance. Some will use it to predict an upside move when the price crosses above a moving average or to exit that trade when the price falls below the moving average. Some may use this indicator to set a trailing stop-loss for their trade. Regardless of how the indicator is applied, it forms flexible support/resistance levels. You can test with different timeframes to find the one that works best with each type of moving average.

Until now, we have discovered some types of support/resistance reflected in different visualized tools and indicators. Within this chapter, it's hard to dig deeply into each of them. Although support/resistance isn't the same as supply/demand (and it will never be), understanding support/resistance helps you to grasp the first cornerstone in the market (which can be found in supply/demand, too): the incessant battle between buyers and sellers.

12

However, support/resistance has its drawbacks, and trading with supply/demand can, for the most part, resolve those issues and open clearer trade opportunities in the financial markets.

Now, let's discover some imperfections in the use of support/resistance levels in determining entry levels.

Imperfections in the use of support/resistance:

1. Missing trades

The first drawback of using support/resistance level is missed opportunities. Take a look at the picture below:

This is the USD/JPY daily chart. To the left of the chart, the price made a strong sell-off from the 112.100, making it a strong resistance level. Not surprisingly, the price tried to come back to the level one month later but just failed to touch the resistance threshold. Any limit order at the resistance level would not be triggered, and traders may miss a 600 pip downward move in the following month.

This situation is not uncommon in any financial market. Traders may console themselves that there will be no negative effect to their trading account if they miss a trade. But no one wants to constantly miss good opportunities again and again. This is why supply/demand will come into place.

## 2. Lagging signals

The second problem with supply/demand trading lies in the mathematical formula-based indicator. A moving average can be easy to use, but it goes behind the price, and provide delayed feedback to users. That's why it is categorized into the lagging indicator group. Any lagging indicator can become a nightmare for traders unless they used them in combination with other trading signals. Moving averages should be considered as a confirmation signal instead of the key to any trading system.

Take a look at the example below:

In this example, at one point, the price broke above the 50-day moving average (MA50), but buyers' strength is short-lived and the price quickly continued its downward movement. This is just one common example that traders may feel deceived by moving average as a support/resistance level.

3.   Break or bounce back

In terms of support/resistance, trend lines are considered a great tool to identify the overall trend in the market. Market participants often expect a successful pullback or break from a support or resistance level to place a trade in the direction of the said pullback or break. However, it's quite hard and risky to predict whether the price will bounce or break when testing any individual trend line. More often than not, traders fail to catch the next right move of the price due to a lot of market chaos occurring frequently. From my experience, a trend line should be used as a confirmation signal instead of a backbone of a trading system, just like moving average.

All the popular support and resistance types above are visualized by specific lines. A common drawback of using a line indicator is the price can miss or pierce through it multiple times, making it difficult for you to determine reliable entry and stop prices. On the other hand, using a "zone" or "area" could be a game-changer. In many books, I emphasize the importance of the price zones for trade purposes. However, many questions arise regarding how to identify and draw a zone, how to assess price zones, how to trade with them, how to manage trades when trading with the zones, etc. All the answers can be found when we learn about **supply and demand trading**, which discloses the momentum behind each price movement and the correlation between the bulls and the bears to help us deliver the best trade decisions.

In the next chapters, we will discuss supply and demand, how they work, and how to use them the most effective so that we can stack the odds in our favor.

# Chapter 2: Introduction of Supply & Demand

## Supply and Demand At First Glance

Supply and Demand are considered fundamental concepts in microeconomics. Put simply, it is the study of the interaction between buyers and sellers to identify the market price (or equilibrium price) and the quantities of the goods or services supplied.

## Supply

Supply describes the total amount of a particular good or service available for purchase at a specific price. When the price rises, producers will manufacture more to cater to buyers' needs and increase revenue. By contrast, when the price falls, they tend to narrow production due to the inability to cover production costs. Therefore, there is a positive correlation between the price and the number of goods or services provided. The picture below illustrates this relationship.

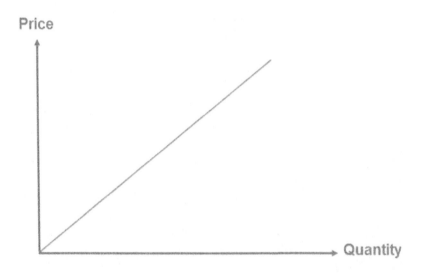

Look at the upward diagonal line. It indicates the quantities of specific goods or services that sellers are willing to sell at each price level within a certain period.

The higher the price is, the bigger the quantity is, and vice versa.

Demand

Demand indicates the number of goods or services that buyers are willing to purchase at a certain price. Understandably, when a product is becoming costly, people tend to look for an alternative product or wait for its price to fall to a more reasonable price level for a buy decision. This causes the demand to drop. Otherwise, when the price of a product drops, buyers tend to believe this is a bargain and will be more interested in buying the product.

To put it simply, the correlation between prices and demand is negative. Take a look at the chart below.

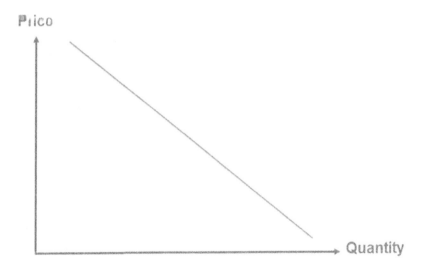

The downward diagonal line illustrates the quantities of specific goods or services that buyers are willing to spend money for at different price levels during a period.

When the supply line and demand line cross, a consensus price or equilibrium price is determined. It is the price that both sides agree for the transaction to be completed at that time.

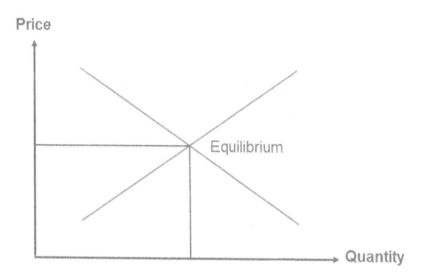

In any market, the equilibrium price is the price where the demand quantity equals the supply quantity. Also, there is only one equilibrium price that can be reached at a single time. In real life, consumers tend to look for a more reasonable price while producers always want to increase the price to better cover production expenses. In any circumstance, a market balance needs to be achieved for a business transaction to be engaged.

Let's take "apple" as an example.

Suppose that it has been a good year for apple farmers with more apples produced than expected. Yet, consumers will be willing to buy just enough, meaning that supply quantity is higher than demand quantity. If apple sellers want to sell out their inventory, they will need to apply some methods to stimulate buyers to take action. One of the easiest and simplest ways of stimulation is by decreasing the apple price. Now, buyers tend to buy more because they can afford a bigger number of apples in the market. In this way, the price will continue to fall until all the apple inventory finds its buyers successfully. That would be the market balance where the demand quantity equals the supply quantity.

Toward the end of the apple season, the farmers clear their inventory quicker and there are a small number of apples left in the market. As the number of shoppers stays the same, less supply will push the price higher. The price will continue to rise until there are enough buyers willing to pay to buy out the remaining apples. Under this market condition, the market has found a new balanced price.

As long as there is enough goods and service to satisfy buyers' needs, the price may not fluctuate widely. Once one side exceeds the other in quantity, for example, there is more demand quantity than the supply quantity, this will result in an *imbalance*. This imbalance will cause prices to fluctuate until it achieves a new balance.

*"Imbalance"* will be the main "keyword" that is repeated many times throughout this book and is the key to trading with supply and demand. More on that later.

## Supply and Demand In Trading

In the financial market, the same principle applies.

When the supply for an asset or instrument is high while the demand is low, this will drag the price lower. In contrast, when the demand exceeds supply, this will drive the price higher until a balance is achieved.

Traders use the law of supply and demand in the financial market to make profits from market imbalances.

The constant interaction between buyers (aka "bulls") and sellers (aka bears) results in the uptrend and downtrend in the market. The bulls always look for the price to fall to consider an advantageous trade entry while the bears do the opposite.

For example, if the economic data reveals that the economy is doing better than expectations, this may stimulate the need for stock in anticipation of higher earnings. Otherwise, during times of recession or uncertainty, investors may reduce their exposure in the equity market and pay more attention to safe-haven currencies, assets, or commodities to protect their investment.

Another example is with the Federal Reserve's decision to increase or decrease interest rate, which often catches the attention of traders in every financial market, especially the Forex market. A decision to increase the interest rates, for example, will make the US dollar more attractive to investors, leading to more demand for the US dollar in the currency market.

Still in the Forex market, since currency pairs don't have an intrinsic value, supply and demand analysis becomes an ideal way to assess the value of a Forex pair.

Let's have a brief look at how pro traders use supply and demand in forex trading.

On this chart, the trend is up and we have several demand areas. Don't worry if you can't figure out how these areas are drawn. Later, we will show you step-by-step the art of trading with these two powerful forces.

Coming back to the chart, traders tend to place buy orders in these areas where buyers outnumber sellers according to the law of supply and demand.

20

Notice that in many cases, the price jumps when it hits the demand zones. The underlying reason behind these jumps is a number of (big) orders from big funds and institutions are waiting to get filled at these areas. Each time the price makes a correction, it tends to bounce back to these demand zones, creating a series of higher highs and higher lows.

If all unfilled orders at a demand area have been absorbed, the price will find other demand areas where buyers exceed sellers. The process continues until buyers don't outnumber sellers anymore.

On the contrary, in a supply zone, sellers exceed buyers, driving the price lower according to the law of supply and demand. Generally, the supply zone, where many sell limit orders are waiting, is positioned above the current price level.

In the chart above, the price tends to visit supply zones on a retracement to match the pending orders. After those orders are filled, the price will move on to find another supply areas where sellers exceed buyers.

## Market Balance – Imbalance In trading

The basic pattern of the market will go like this: balance → imbalance → balance → imbalance. When there is a difference between the supply quantity and demand quantity, an excess is established, and the market will trade in the direction of the predominant side until it reaches a balanced state again. Take a look at the picture below.

### Balance Area

In a balanced market, the number of buyers and sellers is more or less even. This balance paves the way for a quick price consensus and completion of a transaction. As can be seen from the chart, in this type of market, the price often moves in a small range area (no need to make any substantial move to reach a fair level).

### Imbalance Area

Once buyers or sellers gain control of the battle, the market switch to an imbalanced state where the price goes in the direction of the stronger player. If the bulls gain more advantage, the price will climb, otherwise, it will decline.

22

Let's come back to the chart above.

On this chart, we have many arrows pointing at some areas and directions in the market. First, the horizontal arrows show the balance zones. These zones are where both buyers and sellers are active with their trading activities. A consensus price can be reached promptly and the price moves in a tight range.

The diagonal arrows go with the imbalanced stages of the market. Notice how the price often breaks out of the balance zones with a large candlestick, representing a failure to remain balanced in the market. It shows that one side is gaining control and moving the price in their expected direction.

To the left of the chart, the bulls exceed the bears and the price made a substantial climb to find another balance area. Toward the right of the chart, after a substantial drop, the market witnesses smaller-ranged candlesticks (in the rectangle), indicating that market participants are trying to look for another fair price to continue the balanced rotations process.

Trading with supply and demand entails *a correct identification of a balanced zone*, where we place our entry. Then, the following market imbalance will help traders to reap some profits. Simple as that.

The law of supply and demand can apply to a wide variety of things in life. In the financial markets, the dynamics of these two forces result in the determination of the price of an asset/instrument. Professional traders are those who master the art of spotting a tradeable balanced area and patiently monitor the trade during the imbalance stage to make profits.

Mastering supply and demand trading is never a quick and easy process. Don't worry! In the next chapters, I will present everything you need to make the best use of supply and demand analysis in trading, starting with how to identify supply and demand correctly.

# Chapter 3: Spotting The Golden Zone

Trading market imbalances requires the ability to spot the supply and demand zones on a financial chart. These zones are created by large institutions and funds where unfilled orders are waiting to be absorbed. Supply and demand trading boils down to finding smart money in the market. They have the power to affect the price direction on the chart, hence it's safe and advisable to follow them.

Finding a valid supply or demand zone entails following a set of rules closely. In this chapter, we'll go over different patterns of supply and demand before going step-by-step on how to pick up potential supply or demand zones for trading.

## Different patterns of Supply and Demand

Supply and demand areas can be found in two types of patterns on the chart: Reversal and Continuation.

### Reversal

Reversal patterns are formed when there is a change in the trend, either from an uptrend to a downtrend or from a downtrend to an uptrend.

We have two possible patterns in a reversal.

- Drop-Base-Rally: In this pattern, the price is initially in a downtrend, then forms a base before making a rally to the upside.

- Rally-Base-Drop: In this pattern, the price starts with an uptrend before forming a base at the top area of that uptrend. From that base, the price falls, creating a new downtrend.

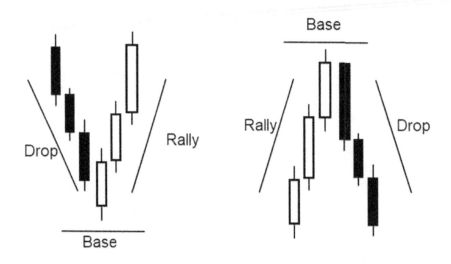

Now, let's take a look at a real example.

On the left side of the chat, we have a rally-base-drop pattern. The price made a strong rally, then stopped for a while, creating a base at the top of the structure. From the top, the price plummeted to the downside. Notice how the drop occurred in a strong fashion, with a large bearish candlestick at the beginning of the downtrend.

Moving gradually to the right of the chart, we have two drop-base-rally patterns. The rallies are also strong ones with the presence of long bullish candlesticks. This indicates clear imbalances in the market.

Continuation

Besides reversal patterns, supply and demand areas appear in a trend continuation as well. In this case, such areas play as a base for the price to test before continuing the overall trend until the strength correlation between the bulls and the bears changes.

There are two continuation patterns:

- Drop-Base-Drop: The price drops, slows for a while on a base, and then continues to fall.

- Rally-Base-Rally: The price increases, slows for a while on a base, and then continues to increase.

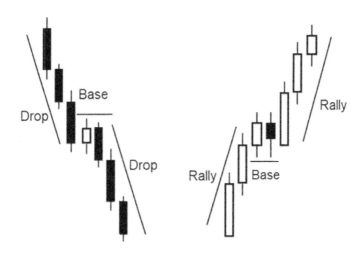

Take a look at a real example.

Unlike the reversal patterns, continuation patterns are found within the trend and are considered weaker than the reversal structure. In trading, we'll give reversal patterns a priority in spotting a potential trade zone. Yet, this doesn't mean we ignore continuation patterns. Although considered not as strong as reversal patterns, continuation patterns are still worth trying in many cases.

Now that we've grasped the necessary fundamentals of two types of patterns where supply and demand zones may appear, let's continue to discover potential supply and demand zones in the next section.

## How to identify Supply and Demand zones

### Market imbalance

Supply and demand zones are closely connected with imbalances, which are characterized by big price movements, either up or down. A market

28

imbalance appears when either buyers or sellers gain control and drive the price a long way from the base with strong momentum.

Looking at the chart below:

- When demand exceeds supply, the price climbs with big bullish candlesticks.
- When supply exceeds demand, the price climbs with big bearish candlesticks.

These price movements indicate where the imbalances are in the market. Any imbalance is a money-making opportunity for traders. In any circumstance, going with the trend from its beginning is the best way to enjoy the most profits from the market move.

One thing to remember here is the presence of *extended-range candlestick* (or ERC). In some examples in this chapter, we've tried to emphasize the importance of ERCs because they provide high probability trade areas on the chart.

Now, let's jump straight to a set of rules in identifying a supply or demand zone.

## Three steps in determining a supply or demand zone

- Step 1: Identify current price

Starting from the current price level, we look to the left of the chart until a big strong move (either up or down) appears. Take a look at the picture below.

- Step 2: Looking for ERCs

Still on the big movement that we've found, determine whether there are ERCs in it or not. ERCs are strong candlesticks with short or no wick. As a rule of thumb, any candlestick whose body occupies more than half of the candlestick's range can be considered an ERCs. Two ERCs would be the minimum requirement for a strong move.

30

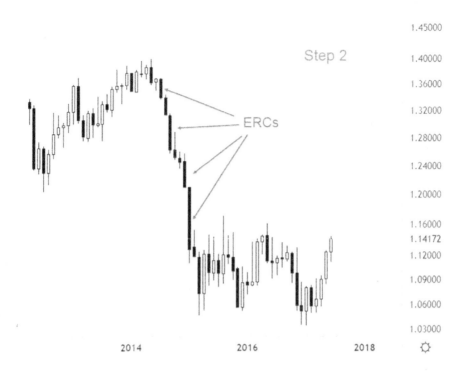

- Step 3: Finding the origin of the big move

The final step in identifying a supply or demand zone is to trace back to the origin of the zone. This area will be where the supply or demand zone is formed. We will learn how to draw the zone step-by-step in the next chapter. For now, take a look at the zone in a rally-base-rally pattern below.

As we can see, the price climbed to the base, paused for a short period before moving down strongly with the presence of some ERCs.

One important note is identifying supply and demand zones should be done from a longer timeframe first, i.e monthly or weekly chart. Soon we will learn about the art of trading with multiple timeframes. Starting with a longer timeframe better filter out the chaos in the markets, and ensure that you are following the dominant trend.

## Examples of supply and demand zones

### Example 1: Continuation pattern

In this example, the price was in a strong downtrend. A strong drop was slowed by a basing structure, then continued with some other big bearish candlesticks. We have a drop-base-drop structure on the chart. Notice how the price retested the supply zone, showing that more unfilled orders at this zone had been waiting to get executed.

## Example 2: Reversal pattern

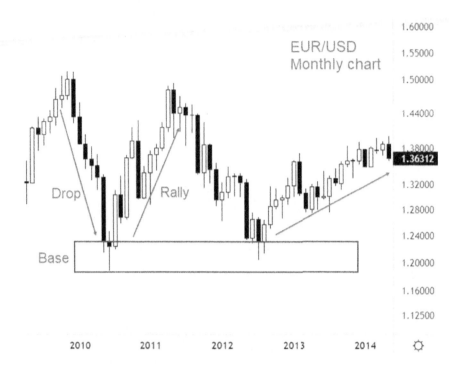

This example illustrates a drop-base-rally type of demand zone. This is a reversal structure where the market changes from a downtrend to an uptrend.

A basing structure was formed to end a strong price decline and to pave the way for a new rally. This rally tells us the buyers dominated the market at that point, however, the price didn't soar straight away. Instead, it revisited the zone for unfilled orders (aka buy limit orders) to get absorbed.

Example 3: Mixed patterns

In this example, we can see a series of patterns of different types. To the left of the chart, a rally-base-rally was present. Moving toward the middle of the chart, we have successive rally-base-drop, drop-base-rally, and rally-base-rally patterns. Mixed structures type of demand or supply are not uncommon in the financial market, and you should train your eyes so that you won't miss any potential trade zones using the law of supply and demand.

In any circumstance, after identifying the zones, all you need to do next is wait for the price to revisit the zone, and then a trade can be triggered shortly.

Identifying supply or demand zones may not be a complex and difficult task, but it is the first task before moving to the next important ones.

One important thing to remember is the presence of the ERCs. The underlying reason behind it is that ERCs reflect the true imbalance in the market, thus increasing the chance of trade profitability. In contrast, a directional move with mostly indecision candlesticks may not indicate a reliable dominance, thus failing to put the odds in our favor. In the next chapter, we'll learn how to draw a supply and demand zone using different methods.

35

# Chapter 4: How To Draw Supply/Demand Zones

Trading supply and demand successfully starts with *identifying* and *drawing* high probability trade zone. The former has been done in the previous chapter. This chapter will focus on the latter, which truly deserves the time spent.

Drawing a supply or demand zone is centered around determining two lines around a basing structure that we mentioned in the previous chapter. Our entry and stop-loss price will then be identified based on this zone. In this chapter, we'll introduce three different ways of drawing a zone to wait for the next price retest.

## Distal and Proximal Line

To draw a supply or demand zone, we need two lines: the proximal line and the distal line. They are the two borders of the basing pattern and form the golden area that we'll use to place initial entry and stop-loss prices.

While the distal line is located at the further end of the zone, the proximal line is positioned at the nearer end of the zone. These two lines are illustrated in the picture below.

| Distal Line | Proximal Line |
|:---:|:---:|
| ———————— | ———————— |
| ———————— | ———————— |
| Proximal Line | Distal Line |
| **Supply Zone** | **Demand Zone** |

An important note to all supply and demand traders that I want to emphasize many times in this book is *not all zones work*. We'll go over multiple criteria in analyzing each zone in the following chapters. Within this chapter, below are some types of candlesticks that might not be ideal for a high-probability trading zone.

A tradable supply or demand zone shouldn't have:

- Several long-tailed candlesticks;
- Staircase candlesticks;
- Doji candlestick only;

First, a zone with several long-tailed candlesticks might be the indication that those candlesticks are just the reaction to a previous basing structure. Take a look at the chart below.

In this example, several candlesticks in a zone are reacting to the previous demand zone. The long shadows indicate that traders went down just to fulfill pending buy limit orders. The price then moved back and forth before a strong enough force can drive the price higher.

Next, a zone in a staircase shape will not be considered a high probability trading zone. This pattern is created by:

- A candlestick closing below the previous candlestick's close in a supply zone;
- A candlestick closing above the previous candlestick's close in a demand zone;

Finally, if the zone is formed by a Doji candlestick only, just pass and move on to the next patterns. The example below illustrates how the price pays little respect to the zone and continues with its direction.

EUR/JPY
Daily chart

125.981
125.603
125.000
124.000
123.000
122.000
121.000
120.000
119.000
118.000
117.000
116.000
115.000
114.100

May          Jun          Jul          Aug

## How to draw supply and demand zones

When it comes to drawing supply and demand areas, each trader may have his/her ways of doing. Some may resort to a specific method of drawing, while others may not have any specific rules of determining the zone. To me, drawing any zone should be based on a set of principles.

In this section, I'll show you three simple methods of drawing the distal and proximal lines depending on your risk tolerance.

### Supply zones

As we learn in previous chapters, a supply zone could be in the type of the rally-base-drop or rally-base-rally shape.

Below are the three ways of drawing a supply zone.

- The medium-risk method

The distal line is located at the highest of the basing structure while the proximal line is placed at the lowest body price of the base.

39

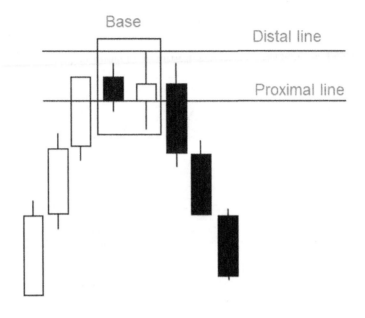

Base

Distal line

Proximal line

- The high-risk method

This method can be preferred by risk-tolerant traders, where the distal line is drawn at the highest price of the base range while the proximal line is at the lowest price of the range. A clear advantage of this method is your pending order can be triggered earlier, and you can avoid missing some good opportunities when trading. However, the stop-loss price is placed further, meaning that you can suffer from a bigger loss compared to other methods.

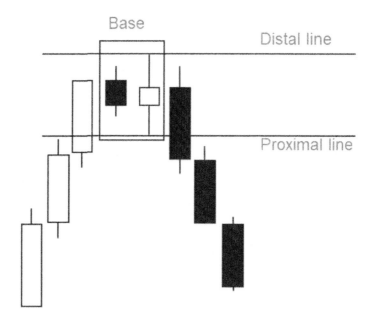

- The low-risk method

This method is more suitable for risk-averse traders. The distal line is placed at the highest price in the base range, and the proximal line is placed at the highest body price in the basing structure. With this method, your entry price wouldn't be as good as in other methods, but the loss would be the most comfortable when triggered.

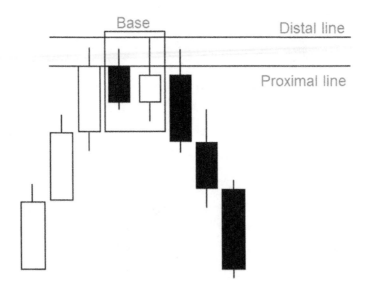

<u>Demand zones</u>

A demand zone can be in the shape of drop-base-rally or drop-base-drop. Drawing the supply zone is based on the same principle but the opposite side.

- The medium-risk method

In this method, the distal line is placed at the lowest price in the basing structure. Meanwhile, the proximal line is placed at the highest body price in the zone.

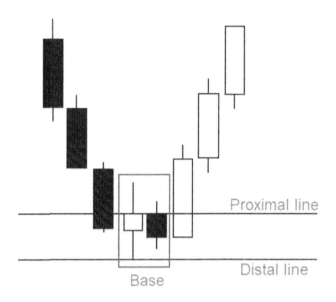

- The high-risk method

The distal line and the proximal line are placed at two price extremes in the demand zone. This method is preferred by risk-tolerant traders. The loss would be the biggest if the stop price is hit, however, traders can have their trades triggered at a better price.

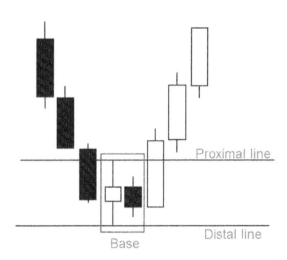

- The low-risk method

Still, the distal line is drawn through the lowest price point in the range. Meanwhile, the proximal line is placed at the lowest body price in the basing structure.

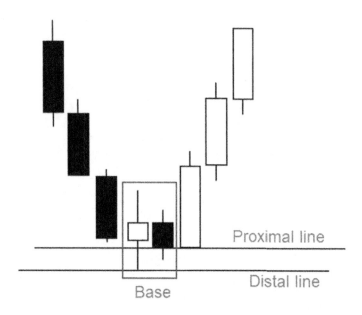

Proximal line

Distal line

Base

Gaps

Gaps are common on financial trading charts. To put it simply, a gap occurs where the open price of a candlestick doesn't equal the close price of the previous one. We will talk more about trading with gaps later in the book. In this section, the main point will be centered around drawing a supply or demand zone.

As a rule of thumb, we always draw the zone *at the origin of the gap*, not the other way round. The picture below will best illustrate this technique.

## Determining entry and exit prices using supply or demand zone

There are two main options in trading with supply or demand zones:

1. Using a market order

Traders are more active with this type of order. Those orders are the simplest trade orders where you place a command to buy or sell an asset/instrument at the currently available price.

Traders often choose this order type as a safe option after they've observed the price fluctuations closely enough (especially around the supply or demand zones) to make a final decision of whether they place an order or not. Also, applying a market order removes the possibility of missing out on good trade opportunities.

We'll talk more about this type of order in Chapter 6.

2. Using limit orders

This is what most examples in this book are based on.

Unlike a market order, a limit order allows you to buy or sell an asset/instrument at a better price than the current price. In other words, a buy limit order allows you to buy at a lower price while a sell limit order allows you to sell at a higher price. With that said, the limit order is not always implemented, depending on whether the price reaches your desired level or not. Limit orders ensure that you won't pay higher in case of a long order and won't sell lower in case of a short order.

Limit orders are preferred when you identify the current price is still not the ideal one for trade execution, and you are not in a rush for entering a trade. For example, you determine that there is a better chance of gold reversing upward when it comes to the $1,700 price level from the current price of $1,900, you'll put a buy limit order at $1,700. If you think the gold price will reverse downward when it reaches $2,000, then a sell limit (or take-profit) order will be placed at $2,000.

There are three limit orders in trading with a supply and demand zone.

- Entry price: Placed at the proximal line
- Stop price: Place just above the distal line (when trading with supply zones), and just below the distal line (when trading with demand zones).
- Take-profit price: Placed at the next opposing zone

Of course, trading is not as easy as identifying the zones and placing some limit orders. The most difficult but exciting part of trading with supply and demand is still ahead.

## Examples of proximal and distal lines

Before discovering techniques and strategies in trading with supply and demand zones, let's look at some real examples of how the proximal and distal lines are drawn on the chart.

### Example 1:

In this example, we have a rally-base-drop pattern, and a demand area should be targeted. As can be seen, the medium-risk method is used in drawing the zone, with the proximal line at the lowest body price and the distal line at the highest price level in the basing structure. Notice how the base includes only two candlesticks, and without the appearance of Doji, staircase, or several long-tailed candlesticks.

EUR/USD
Daily chart

Example 2:

In this example, a strong downtrend was in the shape of a drop-base-drop pattern. The distal line is placed at the highest price of the range and the proximal line is at the lowest body price of the base.

47

Example 3:

In this example, we use the high-risk method in determining the supply zone of the chart. As can be seen, widening the basing structure helps traders to catch the price retest successfully.

Example 4:

In the example below, we have a drop-base-rally pattern. Using a low-risk method, traders could still be able to catch the retest of the market price. The proximal line and the distal line are located at the lowest body price and the lowest range price respectively.

The example below presents a rally-base-rally structure, in which the base consists of two candlesticks. The distal line is at the lowest price level of the zone, while the proximal line would either be at the highest zone price or the highest candlestick body price.

As we can see, whichever method we choose, we can still catch the price drop for a retest.

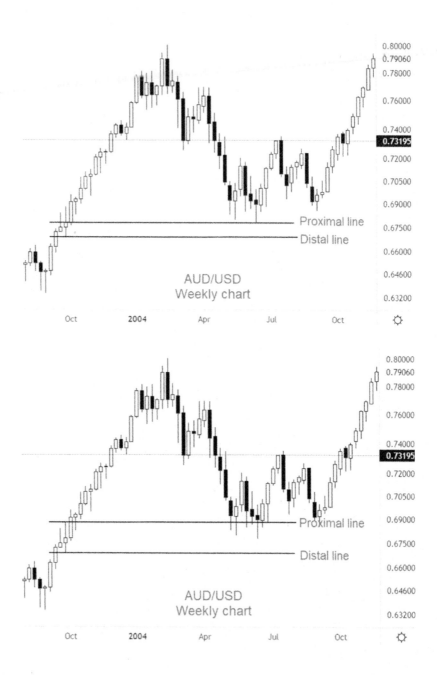

Example 6:

This example illustrates a drop-base-rally structure. By choosing a conservative (low-risk) method of drawing the demand zone, we can still be able to catch the retest where unfilled orders quickly got filled. The price then rallied up quite smoothly.

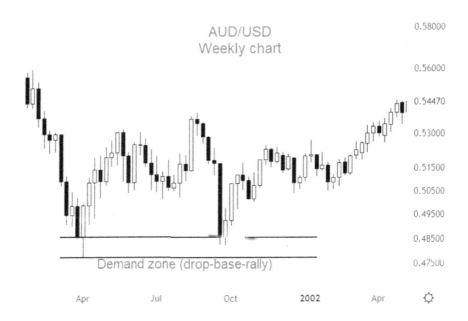

Drawing supply and demand zones seems quite simple where it all boils down to correctly identifying the two important horizontal lines. However, in a real chart, it might not be always easy to define a trade zone due to high market volatilities, which sometimes cause a mess on the trading chart. We'll mention some other treasured tips in identifying a tradable zone in the following chapters, which might help you cope with those volatilities on the chart.

For now, keep in mind that it requires a lot of practice to figure out where to place the proximal lines and distal lines. But once you can master the price zone, the next steps will become much more comfortable implementing.

Spend time in front of the trading chart, be patient, and start looking for the supply and demand zone.

The next two chapters will partly help you explain the reason for a lot of losses incurred in trading.

51

# Chapter 5: Always Stick To The Best

One of the myths about trading is the more trades you take, the more profits you'll make. On any financial chart, we can easily spot a lot of trade setups or candlestick patterns. So why do most traders fail again and again?

The answer is simple: **high probability**. Professional traders always try to optimize their trade entry so that they can have a higher chance of taking a successful trade. They only place a trade where a number of criteria are satisfied.

Things are not different in trading with supply and demand. Not every supply or demand zone is tradable. If you scan the history of any asset or instrument, you can see that a lot of zones fail to work. In this chapter, I will present one important concept and if you stick to it, you can avoid a lot of risky trades.

## Fresh and original zones

A fresh zone is a supply or demand area that has not been tested yet. While it isn't a compulsory condition, trading decisions should be based on fresh levels. When a zone has not been visited, many pending orders are still waiting there, and the chance for a successful retest, to some extent, is high.

An original zone is a supply or demand area that is formed out of nowhere. In contrast, if the zone is created as a reaction of a previous supply or demand zone, it is not original.

When a zone is formed out of nowhere and has not been tested yet, it is an original and fresh zone. This is an ideal zone to consider trading before taking other odd enhancers into consideration to decide whether to trade or not.

## How to determine a fresh zone?

Below are three simple steps in determining whether a zone is fresh or not.

- We start by identifying the zone in control (this is learned in the previous chapters).
- Determine where the zone has been retested or not.

- If there has not been any retest, the zone is fresh. Otherwise, if there is at least one retest, the zone is not fresh anymore.

On the chart above, we have two demand zones formed in the type of rally-base-rally patterns. These zones are not fresh ones because they are all tested. Two circles on the chart show how price revisited these areas. Trading these zones may put traders in a vulnerability of a zone breakthrough.

The next chart illustrates both fresh and non-fresh zones. We have three supply areas and one demand area on this chart. Again, we move our eyes from the left to the right to see whether these zones have been tested or not.

The two upper fresh zones are fresh because there has been no retest on them. These areas might have a large number of pending orders waiting to be triggered. As mentioned, they offer a better prospect for your trade. Hence, we should pay more attention to these levels.

The lowest supply zone is not fresh because the price has returned and broke above the proximal line once.

Likewise, the only demand zone in this example is not fresh. The price has retraced back down and touched the proximal line.

### How to determine an original zone?

Identifying an original zone also includes three steps, but there is a small difference. Here is how:

- We start by identifying a supply or demand zone, using the techniques we've learned in the previous chapters (let's call zone 1).
- From the zone we've identified, continue to move our eyes horizontally to the left of the chart until a candlestick appears.
- If the candlestick is part of a supply or demand zone (zone 2), zone 1 is not original. Otherwise, it is an original zone.

54

Now, take a look at some examples to see what the technique looks like in real trading.

In the example above, we have a demand zone with the proximal line and distal line plotted. From the zone, we look back to history and quickly find a long bullish candlestick. This candlestick is part of an imbalance phase instead of a basing structure. It means that the zone in consideration is not a reaction of any other previous zone. In other words, it is original.

Let's move to another chart.

Original, non-fresh zone

GBP/JPY
4-hour chart

In this example, a supply zone is formed in a rally-base-drop pattern. Once again, we move to the left until being blocked by two big bearish candlesticks. They are not part of any previous zone, hence the zone in consideration is original, too. Also, note that it was tested once, hence is not a fresh zone.

In the long run, fresh and original zones will help you in filtering out some risky areas in trading. A fresh zone implies that there are many pending orders to be absorbed, and the chance of success is somewhat higher than when the zone has been tested two or three times. The same explanation applies to an original zone.

Keep in mind that these are not hard and fast rules, and they aren't strict guidelines to follow at all costs. We can also see non-fresh zones still generate very good signals of a reversal. However, the idea across this book is to focus on the best signals only to achieve a higher winning rate. The next chapter will provide much more tips and techniques to help us better optimize our supply and demand trade zone.

# Chapter 6: Tradable Or Not?

This chapter will focus on one concept which may be strange to many traders: the scoring system. We'll learn about using a quantitative measurement to define how tradable your identified zone is in trading. Using a system to calculate a final score of the trading zone helps traders to gain a better view of the zone in control, and remove emotional decisions. A lot of odd enhancers will be featured to calculate a score of the zone, from that we will deliver our trading decisions more confidently and effectively.

## Why score supply and demand zones?

If you have certain experience in trading, spotting a tradable zone is not an easy task, especially when multiple zones are located beside each other. Determining a low-probability trading zone not only results in a potential loss but can also be frustrating and time-consuming.

A scoring system is a system that is developed to filter out low-probability supply or demand zones. By analyzing the following odd enhancers and summarizing the total score of all these enhancers, you increase the winning probability for your trades.

## Odd enhancer in trading with supply and demand

Simply put, an odd enhancer in trading with supply and demand is a filter to give your trade area a higher winning probability. It stacks the odds in your favor. For each of the four compulsory odd enhancers presented below, a scoring system from 0 to a maximum of 3 will be assigned depending on the performance of the zone. The final sum of the five enhancers' scores will let you decide whether to take action or not.

## Compulsory enhancers

We will start with 4 compulsory enhancers. By "compulsory", I mean you should always take these factors into consideration.

<u>Odd enhancer 1: Strength of the move</u>

The first criterion in assessing a trade zone is how strongly the price left the supply or demand zone.

If the price moved out of the zone in a strong fashion, this indicates a strong imbalance. The price quickly moves in the direction of the predominant players, and many unfulfilled orders might stay at the zone waiting to be executed later.

Otherwise, a weak and slow departure from the zone (normally characterized with indecision candlesticks) may imply that orders have been gradually absorbed, and there might not be many pending ones to be fulfilled.

Based on a scoring table of 2, we have three ways of giving a score as shown in the picture below.

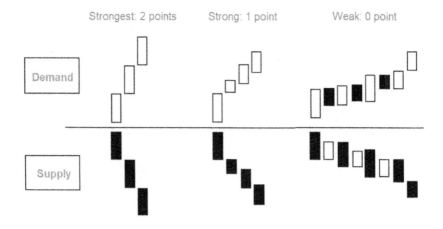

Now, let's move to some examples to better understand the importance of this technique.

On this chart, a supply zone is presented. Look at how the price moved away from the zone with a very long bearish candlestick, showing a great imbalance. When the price visited the zone for the first time, it quickly moved back down. Traders placing a sell limit order at the proximal line of the zone would have made a good decision.

| | 1.36000 |
| | 1.35500 |
| | 1.35100 |
| | 1.34700 |
| | 1.34300 |
| | 1.33900 |

Weak: 0 point

1.33500
1.33382
1.33100
1.32700

GBP/USD
4-hour chart

1.32300
1.31900

14:00    15    14:00    22    25

In this example, a demand zone can easily be identified in a drop-base-rally pattern. However, the price left the zone in a weak fashion with small and medium-sized candlesticks, suggesting that the ascending momentum isn't strong enough, and there might not be many pending orders left at the zone. In other words, buyers are losing interest and are prepared to pass the game control through sellers. As you can see, soon after leaving the zone, the price reversed and moved all the way down, breaking the demand zone in control.

Odd enhancer 2: Time at the zone

This is a very important factor when we analyze the potential of a zone. Each time you spot a trade zone, ask yourself this question: how long did the price stay at the zone?

As a rule of thumb, a zone having at least 6 candlesticks shows a solid balance between the bulls and the bears. If a balanced state remains long, most orders are fulfilled and the chances for a successful retest are not quite high. Hence, once the number of candlesticks in a zone exceeds 5, you can pass that zone and look for another one.

In contrast, a small number of candlesticks in the zone (ideally from one to three) shows a strong imbalance, and there are more unfilled orders waiting to be executed in the future. Think about it, if the imbalance is strong enough, the price will have no reason to spend a lot of time at the zone.

Below is the scoring system based on the price's stay length at the zone.

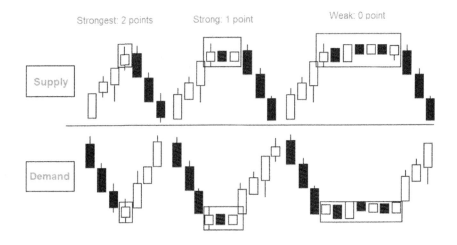

Let's take a look at what a strong zone and a weak zone look like using the second odd enhancer.

In this example, we have one demand zone and one supply zone.

Regarding the demand zone, one positive factor is that the price left in a very strong manner, with two consecutive big bullish candlesticks. However, when looking inside the zone, we can see a lot of candlesticks accumulated, meaning that it is not a strong zone. Look at how the price tested this area but failed to make a rally-up. Instead, it broke through the zone to the downside where there are more unfilled orders waiting to get executed.

Unlike the demand area, the supply zone is a strong one with only one candlestick at the basing structure. The price paid respect to the zone and moved all the way down as soon as it tested it.

Odd enhancer 3: Fresh zone or not

We've learned about it in the previous chapter. A fresh level is what we aim for in every trade although I don't refute the fact that trading non-fresh levels could sometimes bring about winning trades. Remember we're trying to optimize our trade entry instead of placing a perfect trade with a 100% winning probability.

With that said, a fresh zone will be scored 3. If the price retraces to the zone once, the score will be down to 1.5.

If the price tests the zone at least twice, we'll give it a score of 0. At this point, there is hardly any pending order, and trading the zone will become riskier. Just stay on the sidelines and wait for other signals.

In this example, we have a fresh demand zone in the drop-base-rally pattern at the bottom of the chart. Located above are two non-fresh zones. Each of these areas witnesses two price tests, making them more vulnerable to price breakthrough to the downside.

Considering this, the fresh zone will receive 2 points and these two non-fresh zones will receive zero points.

## Odd enhancer 4: Risk/Reward Ratio

This is what I mentioned in nearly every book I've written. It is the ratio calculated by dividing the potential loss amount by the potential profit amount.

For example, if you risk $100 in your trade in return for a potential profit of $400, then the risk/reward is 1:4.

To make things simple, suppose the entry price is placed at the proximal line, stop-loss is at the distal line, and the take-profit price is at the next opposing zone. More on that when we discuss trading techniques.

In trading with supply and demand, I recommend a ratio of at least 1:3 (potential profit is at least 3 times bigger than the risked amount), where we will give the zone 2 points.

If the ratio is from 1:1.5 to 1:2, we'll give the zone 1 point (not recommended).

If the ratio is less than 1:1.5, we give the zone zero (0) point and ignore it.

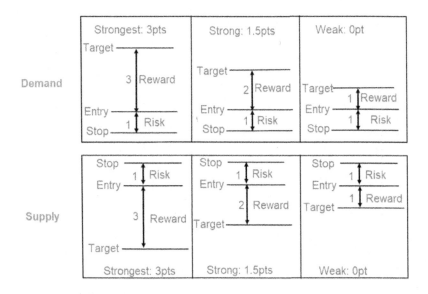

Let's look at some examples below:

In this example, the supply zone in control provides a 1:3 risk/reward ratio, which is worth our attention. Trading based on an ideal ratio like this opens more room for the price to go, thus increasing your profit and benefiting you in the long term.

In this example, the price is kept in a small range between two zones, The risk/reward ratio is only 1:1.3. We can quickly pass this zone and look for another one.

## Optional Enhancers

Besides the enhancers that we need to consider in each of our trades, two other conditions are not mandatory for scoring purposes, but once satisfied, it would boost our confidence in trading. The reason I don't put these enhancers into the compulsory group is to keep everything simple enough for a trade decision. Using too many enhancers may cause the scoring process to become more complicated than needed.

Having said that, once these conditions are met, you'll be much more confident in placing your limit order.

### Odd enhancer 5: Original Zones

This is another concept we've learned in the previous chapter. By "original", we aim at trading a zone created out of nowhere, not a reaction of a previous supply or demand zone.

In this example, we have a demand zone in control. By moving our attention back to the chart history, we see two strong candlesticks which belong to no previous zone. This means that the price zone in consideration is original, and we are stacking the odds in our favor.

Odd enhancer 6: Overlapping Zones

The last enhancer in our list is the overlapping of the zones (also called the nesting zone). It means at least two zones plotted via different timeframes are overlapped, creating a confluence effect as you may already know.

The main idea is that zones from a longer timeframe are stronger than ones that are created in a shorter timeframe. This is one of the biggest secrets in trading with supply and demand. More on that later.

Trading with overlapping zones is not compulsory but is recommended.

Take a look at the following example.

In this example, we have a supply area on the daily chart nested inside the weekly supply area. In any circumstance, you should refer to the longer timeframe first (in this case – the weekly chart) and find a zone. Then, you switch to a shorter timeframe (the daily one) and determine if there is any zone which is overlapped with the bigger one.

## How to score supply and demand zones

Now that we've identified a number of enhancers to consider in our trades, let's determine when we can say "yes" and when we should say "no" to a supply and demand setup.

### A score of 10 points

A score of 10 points means that the zone satisfies every compulsory condition for a trade to be placed. The zone is fresh, with no more than 5 candlesticks in it, having candlesticks leaving in a strong fashion, and provides a good risk/reward ratio.

### A score between 7 and 9 points and no enhancer receive a zero

A score between 7 and 9 points means the zone still has some flaws but is still tradable with a certain winning probability.

There are two ways to trade these zones:

- Using a market order

When a trader uses a market order, he/she wait for the price to close inside the trade zone. The entry price will be placed at the close of the piercing candlestick.

68

- Using a confirmation order

This method is considered less risky compared to the market order. Using this option, we will wait for the price to pierce inside the zone before reversing back above the proximal line with a strong bullish candlestick (the momentum candlestick). An entry price is placed at the close of the momentum candlestick.

Let's take this chart for the illustration.

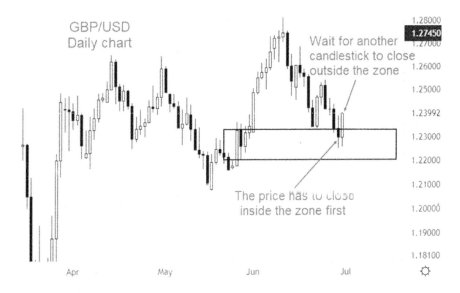

On this chart, we won't enter any trade until the price breaks above the proximal line successfully (ideally with a long bullish candlestick).

A score below 7 points

If the score is below 7, trading with the zone becomes risky. In these cases, just stay away from trading and look for clearer signals.

**Examples**

In this section, we'll go over two different trade zone examples and analyze whether they can be used in trading or not.

The supply zone on this chart is a perfect example to trade. Notice how the price strongly departed from the zone, so we give it 2 points. Second, the base includes only two candlesticks, which once again gives it a maximum score (2). Third, it is 100% fresh (3 points). And finally, the distance from this zone to the opposing demand zone is big enough for a great risk/reward ratio (3 points). All in all, the final score is 10 and this is a good zone to consider placing a limit order.

Now, let's switch to another example.

1. Strength of the move: 1pt
2. Time at the base: 0 pt
3. Fresh zones: 3pts
4. Risk/reward ratio: 1.5 pts

Total: 5.5 pts

Supply zone

Opposing demand zone

0.69600
0.69200
0.68800
0.68400
0.68183
0.68000
0.67600
0.67200
0.66850
0.66500

Sep          Oct          Nov          Dec

In this example, we analyze the trade probability of a supply zone. First, the price broke below the zone with a strong bearish candlestick, followed by some small and medium-sized ones, so we give it 1 point. Second, there are 6 candlesticks at the basing pattern, hence the score is zero (0). Next, the zone has three more points because it has not been touched yet (being fresh). Finally, the risk/reward is approximately 1:2, hence we give it 1.5 points. The total score is 5.5, and traders should be out.

So, in this chapter, we've gone through 6 different zone optimization criteria, of which 4 are for scoring purposes. Traders paying close attention to these enhancers stand a good chance of identifying a high probability trade zone and minimizing the possibility of picking up the wrong supply or demand zones.

I hope the last two chapters have brought you some great ideas about trade optimization. By applying these odd enhancers, you can even look back to your trading history and easily explain the reasons for your losing trades.

Before exploring a lot of strategies and techniques in the next chapters, let's discover a powerful *"trading assistant"* that can make trading with supply and demand zones much easier and more comfortable. This "assistant" can point out potential trading zones and even draws the zones for you. Moreover, you have the chance to improve your skills and techniques by interacting with many other active traders. Most interestingly, this assistant provides you with a fantastic tool to measure the effectiveness of your strategies for as little as zero (0) cents.

All you need is to visit https://bit.ly/3xRgBOg to download for FREE.

Enjoy it!

# Chapter 7: The Price Action's Messages

Price action has been the cornerstone in technical analysis for a long time regardless of which assets or instruments you are trading. Price action technique is the analysis of the price's behaviors over a certain period. The analysis process is done via a clean and simple chart, normally without complicated indicators. Price action trading is preferred by a lot of professional traders thanks to its simplicity and effectiveness.

One of the most important backbones of price action reading is candlestick patterns such as pin bar, head & shoulders, or double top/bottom. In the following section, we'll show you some patterns to watch out for when the price is approaching a basing structure. Combining these patterns with the supply or demand zone would increase the probability of a winning trade.

## Pin bars

A pin bar is a type of candlestick with a small body and a long tail/shadow. The formation of pin bars signals a strong rejection in the price

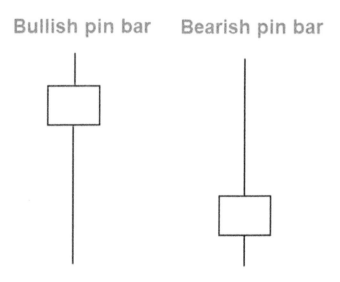

Bullish pin bar      Bearish pin bar

An ideal scenario to look for is when the price tests a supply or demand zone with the presence of on pin bar presented at the proximal line. This indicates that the market momentum is shifting and an imminent reversal is expected shortly. A pin bar could be treated as a confirmation signal in this case. Let's look at the following chart.

In this example, we have a fresh supply zone. Notice how the price was in a nice uptrend before forming a pin bar pattern at this supply zone on the first test. This indicates a shift in the market sentiment and initiated a downtrend afterward.

Keep in mind that not all pin bars work, and blindly entering a trade on the close of a pin bar would serve to blow up your account. In my book "Secrets on reversal trading", I clearly illustrate how to explore shorter timeframes in analyzing the real market structure behind the scene. You can refer to the book by visiting https://amzn.to/3w8xvHc.

## Inside bars

By definition, an inside bar is a candlestick that is fully engulfed by the previous one as shown in the picture below.

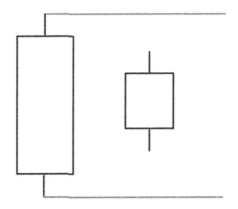

Traders can choose to trade against the trend or trend-following with an inside bar. Take the following chart as an example.

We have three inside bar patterns on this chart. The first one is located near the demand zone, showing a reversal signal of the trend. Trading this inside bar is safer since it is positioned just above the demand zone.

The second bar is formed at the basing structure of a trend continuation (rally-base-rally). This is where you can choose to place an order if you've missed the first opportunity.

The third bar also plays as a continuation pattern. However, at this point, the price is near a supply zone, hence, it is advisable not to enter any trade after the formation of this pattern. Instead, we should wait for the next price actions.

## Head and shoulders

A typical head and shoulders pattern includes three peaks, in which the middle peak is higher than the next two ones. While this pattern is formed during an uptrend, the inverted pattern is formed at the end of a downtrend, initiating an uptrend afterward.

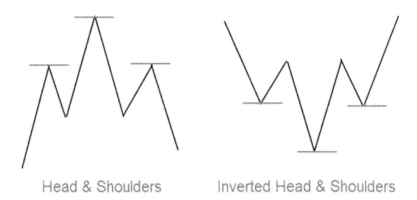

Head & Shoulders        Inverted Head & Shoulders

Again, entering a trade just because a head and shoulder pattern appears could be a very risky decision. When you combine this pattern with a backup of a supply or demand zone, the winning probability is higher.

In this example, an inverted head and shoulder pattern is formed at a demand zone. We have two options:

- 1st option - conservative method: Wait for the price to form a complete head and shoulders pattern and to break the neck of the pattern to enter a long position.
- 2nd option - aggressive method: Wait for the price to form the inverted head and move back out the demand zone to obtain the first clue of a trend reversal. A buy limit order is then placed at the price level equal to the left shoulder. When the price retraces back to form the second shoulder, our pending order gets executed with a stop-loss just below the distal line of the demand zone.

## Double top/bottom

Double top/bottom is a common chart pattern that is characterized by two consecutive tops or bottoms at the end of a trend.

A typical double top pattern has two consecutive highs at a similar price level. This structure is formed at the end of an uptrend.

77

A typical double bottom pattern has two consecutive lows at a similar price level. This pattern is formed at the end of a downtrend.

Keep in mind that by stating "similar", I mean these two tops or bottoms don't have to locate at the same price level. Honestly, it's even better if the second top is a little lower, and the second bottom is a little higher than the first one. This indicates that the reversal momentum has become clear and stronger.

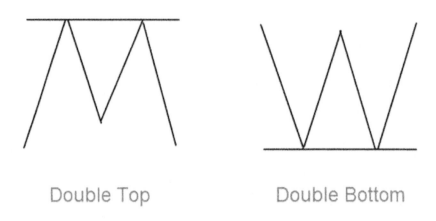

Double Top          Double Bottom

Let's look at the chart below.

In this example, we have a demand zone where a double bottom pattern is identified. Notice after a long downward move, the price found the zone and the downtrend slowed for a period. An uptrend was formed, but it wasn't until another retest at the demand zone (the double bottom was formed) that the price officially left the zone and was ready for a stronger upward move.

Again, not all double top/bottom patterns work all the time. Breaking down a double top/bottom pattern in smaller timeframes could be a great way to gain a better understanding of what the market is telling. This is called the art of market structure analysis that pinged me an aha moment in trading with reversal trading patterns. If you want a deeper analysis of what a reliable change in the market structure looks like, refer to my best-selling book "Secrets on reversal trading".

## Engulfing pattern

The last price action pattern in the list is engulfing candlestick.

An engulfing pattern is commonly spotted when a trend is about to end and the opposite trend starts. A typical example of this pattern includes two candlesticks, in which the second candlestick moves in an opposite direction of the previous one and engulfs that candlestick. An engulfing pattern can appear both in an uptrend and a downtrend. Let's look at a visual illustration of a bullish engulfing pattern below (the bearish one is completely similar but on the opposite side).

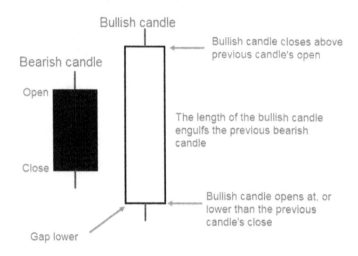

From my observation, engulfing candlesticks appear much more often on the chart compared to other candlestick patterns. By focusing on this pattern, you can spot a lot of good trade opportunities as long as you put the patterns in a bigger picture.

Combining engulfing candlesticks with a supply and demand zone is a perfect option in trading with the zone. Take a look at the following chart.

On this chart, we have a fresh supply zone formed to the left of the chart. Notice that there's only one candlestick at the base, and the price left the zone in a super-powerful manner, not to mention that the risk/reward ratio is exceptional (huge area between the two zones). A very quick glance can tell us this supply zone is well-worth our attention for a short trade.

With the confirmation of a bearish engulfing pattern at the basing structure, we would be much more confident in a positive outcome of the trade. From the supply area, the price hardly had any difficulty in moving all the way down to the opposing zone.

So, we've scanned through five different powerful price action candlestick patterns, which can easily be seen in any volatile market. Remember supply or demand zones are potential places for strong price moves as a result of a market imbalance. An imbalance in the market, in return, is a favorable condition for a rejection or reversal to form. Trading with supply and demand could be much easier and more effective with the help of price action patterns.

81

# Chapter 8: Flip Zones

Supply and Demand Trading has a lot to do with zones identification and optimization. While we should always stick to the scoring system to filter out some lower probability zones from our list, there are other ways to optimize the zones that we should pay attention to. In this chapter, we'll learn about one concept that might be familiar to traders using traditional support/resistance, but is customized to suit supply and demand trading: the flip zone.

## What is a flip zone?

A flip zone is an area where the price flips from support to resistance or vice versa. This concept is derived from the traditional support/resistance trading when a broken support level can turn into a resistance where the price comes back later, and vice versa.

When the price flips from support to resistance, a demand zone is canceled out and a supply zone is formed.

When the price flips from resistance to support, a supply zone is canceled out and a demand zone is formed.

Let's look at two examples below.

EUR/USD
Daily chart

In this example, notice the price tested the support level multiple times before successfully breaking to the downside. The price then came back to test the level, which had turned into a resistance level.

EUR/USD
1-hour chart

In this example, the price tested the horizontal resistance twice before breaking to the upside, flipping the level from resistance to support. The price then came back to test this support multiple times.

In supply and demand trading, we don't focus on a specific price level for our trade decision process, but a zone or a price range. In the next section, we'll go over how we can trade flip zones using the supply and demand theories.

## How to trade using flip zones

### Supply zone flips into Demand zone

Once the price visits a supply area and breaks through it, this shows the probability of the price continuing higher, not the other way round. It means that you should be in a position for a buy entry when the price comes back to the broken zone.

Once you've spotted a flip zone, you'll need to identify and draw a demand zone around the flip level and wait for a retest at the zone. Normally, the price won't go straight up right away without a retest on the zone.

The next chart illustrates how the price successfully formed a flip zone and made a pullback down to the newly created demand zone.

Below is another example.

To the left of the chart, we have a supply zone. On the second test, the zone is pierced through, paving the way for the price to continue its rally.

Notice the resistance flipped into support, but not on the same level. Traders need to be more patient to identify a tradable demand zone in this case.

The newly formed demand zone is created a little higher than the broken resistance level. Yet, by practicing patience, traders are still able to catch the pullback to this demand area and place a long entry.

Demand zone flips into Supply zone

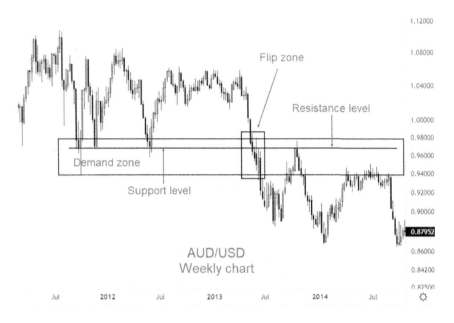

When the price tests a demand zone and successfully breaks below it, the demand zone is officially canceled out and we should watch out for sell opportunities around the broken zone. To do this, we need to identify a newly formed supply zone around the flip area, draw both lines of the zone, and wait for the price to come back for a retest.

As you can see from the chart above, the price did return to the newly formed supply zone and from that, it bounced back down considerably. The initial demand zone was then officially flipped to a supply area.

*Flip zone* brings about another idea of trading with supply and demand. When a supply zone is canceled out, there is a chance that it might change into a demand zone, and vice versa. A successful trader should be quick at determining whether there is a shift in the market sentiment or not. When a flip zone occurs, it means that the overall trend is still valid, and traders should consider going with the dominant trend. Placing a trade around the flipped level could also be a great idea of adding another position using the supply and demand techniques.

# Chapter 9: Reversal and Continuation Trading with Supply/Demand

In Chapter 3, we've learned some reversal and continuation structures in trading with supply and demand. Reversal and continuation are the two basic patterns that we base in identifying supply and demand areas on the chart. In this chapter, we'll go over a few rules and techniques in trading with reversal and continuation structures.

## Reversal pattern trading

In terms of supply and demand trading, a reversal is characterized by a rally-base-drop or drop-base-rally pattern.

The rally-base-drop is formed at the end of an uptrend before the price shifts to a downtrend.

The drop-base-rally is formed at the end of a downtrend before the price shifts to an uptrend.

The following chart illustrates both a drop-base-rally (at the bottom of the chart) and the rally-base-drop (at the top of the chart).

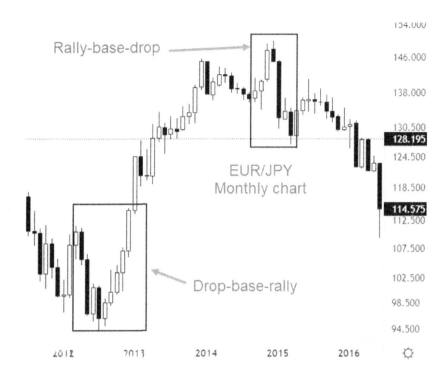

Rally-base-drop

Drop-base-rally

EUR/JPY
Monthly chart

When the trend is over-extended, we watch out for a reversal pattern to occur. As a rule of thumb, once the price has completed more than 3 consecutive continuation structures, it is considered over-extended.

Look at the chart below:

To the left of this chart, the price formed a supply zone in the type of a rally-base-drop pattern. It continued to create four consecutive continuation patterns before the downward momentum became weaker.

After the 4th continuation structure, the price failed to form another continuation pattern and established a bottom at B. From this point, it broke the trend line, forming a new demand zone in the type of drop-base-rally pattern. A new uptrend officially started at the trough.

Identifying reversal patterns

- In an uptrend

The price forms a head and shoulders pattern (the W shape) at the peak of the chart. Look at the chart below:

From A, the price forms the 3<sup>rd</sup> continuation pattern and increases to B.

In B, the price reaches the highest high and forms a new supply area at the peak of the chart.

In C, the price corrects back up to test the nearest supply zone (the first continuation pattern in the downtrend) and continues to move lower.

- In a downtrend

The price forms an inverted head and shoulders pattern (the "M" shape) at the trough of the chart. Look at the example below.

From A, the price forms the 3rd continuation pattern and then drops down to B.

In B, the price reaches the lowest low during the process and creates a new demand zone at the trough of the chart.

In C, the price makes a pullback down before starting a strong rally-up.

How to trade reversal patterns

Principle: We wait for the price to correct back to the first continuation structure for a trade entry.

Let's take the following example:

On the monthly chart, the price is in an over-extended mode with more than three consecutive patterns. We should be in a position to buy the currency pair. Now, let's switch to the weekly chart.

On the weekly chart, the ascending trend line is broken, opening a clearer window for a short entry. Below is the daily chart of the same pair.

On the daily chart, the price also broke the trend line and formed a new supply zone at the top of the chart. Soon the price formed the first continuation pattern.

To trade this W pattern, we wait for the price to come back to the first continuation pattern for a short entry. Trading on the first retest gives us a large enough room for the price to move.

Whereas, after the third continuation pattern, we shouldn't take the risk since the trend momentum has become much weaker.

## Continuation pattern trading

Continuation patterns are created inside the trend. Compared to reversal patterns, continuation patterns are less ideal to trade. Yet, they're still worth considering when they appear at the beginning of a trend, or just after the formation of a reversal pattern. It's when there is a lot of trending momentum ahead and enough room for the price to make a big move.

<u>Identifying continuation patterns</u>

Continuation patterns include rally-base-rally and drop-base-drop structures.

In an uptrend, the price forms consecutive rally-base-rally structures.

In a downtrend, the price forms consecutive drop-base-drop structures.

Take a look at the chart below where a downtrend continuation pattern is in place. A series of drop-base-drop patterns are formed throughout the trend.

<u>How to trade continuation patterns</u>

***Principle 1:*** The trend must be valid. If the descending trend line is broken (in an uptrend) or the ascending trend line is broken (in a downtrend), just remain on the sidelines. As far as the trend is held and the price respects the trend line, we should be in a position to place a trade.

***Principle 2:*** If the price creates more than 3 continuation patterns, we stay out of the trade. 3 CPs means that price has become over-extended and is no longer valid for a trade consideration. After the third pattern, there might be potential trend line breakout waiting and we should be in a position for a reversal trade at that point.

96

The best period to trade a continuation pattern is within the first three CPs in a trend. This is when the trend momentum is strong and the chance of a reversal of the market is limited. Among the three CPs, always aim at the first one, which often occurs soon after the reversal pattern.

Take a look at the example below:

In this example, we have an inverted head and shoulders pattern and we look for a buy trade. Notice how the price respects the descending trend line and we should be in a position for a buy trade.

Once a demand zone was created at the bottom of the chart, the price continued to move higher with 3 continuation patterns. After the third CP, the price moved in a sideways range for a period before plummeting to the downside.

In short, there are two types of supply and demand patterns: continuation and reversal. While the continuation patterns appear inside and throughout the trend, the reversal patterns are located at the end of the trend.

Trading these reversal and continuation patterns entails determining whether we have a W pattern or an M pattern. Moreover, whether a trend line is broken or respected could tell us something about the health of the trend, and is a good indicator for our decision-making process. A perfect price range for trading is from the first CP to the third CP. After the third CP, the trend is considered over-extended and we should be prepared for a reversal trade.

# Chapter 10: Gap Trading With Supply and Demand

In the financial markets, gaps are often created on weekends when most markets are temporarily closed. Also, they can occur right after economic news releases when prices tend to jump quicker and stronger than normal.

One common mistake among many traders is they trade *in the direction of the gap*. For example, if a gap down appears, they blindly short the asset with the assumption that the price would continue to fall. This is among the most severe mistakes in trading with gaps. Those traders would soon feel betrayed by the market and would not believe in the gap trading anymore.

With the help of supply and demand theory, gap trading becomes easier to adopt. It entails a clear identification of whether those gaps are ending or starting ones, then applying the super-technique on supply and demand trading to determine a suitable trade entry.

In this chapter, we'll learn about what a gap is, the difference between a starting gap and an ending gap, and most importantly, how to combine gaps with supply and demand in trading

## Gaps

By definition, a gap is a space between the close of one candlestick and the open of the following candlestick. It is caused by an abrupt price move without any trading taking place within that space. When a gap is created above the previous candlestick's close, it's called a gap up. Whereas, if the gap is created beneath the previous candlestick's close, it's called a gap down.

Gaps are more commonly spotted in stock trading than in other types. Gaps in stock charts are derived from earning reports or any other economic and financial events. In other markets, for example, the forex market, a gap can be the result of an interest rate adjustment or other major releases of economic statistics.

Let's take a look at the following Forex chart to see what a gap looks like.

Gap

GBP/USD
4-HOUR CHART

14:00          14          14:00          21          28          ☼

On this chart, a gap occurred over the weekend. The price went all the way down from 1.3500 to 1.3400, creating a 100-pip gap down on the chart.

## Ending and Starting Gaps

In trading, we have two main types of gaps: ending and starting.

While the starting gap is formed in the opposite direction of the prevailing trend, the ending gap is formed in the direction of the prevailing trend.

Understanding these two types of gaps saves traders from blindly placing a trade in the direction of the gaps. In the next section, you will see how patience does help us in trading with gaps effectively.

First, let's look at two examples of an ending gap and a starting gap.

On the left chart, a gap is spotted during an uptrend. The price makes a sharp move to the upside, creating an empty space. Moving to the right, another gap occurs, but in the opposite direction of the trend (strong uptrend) at that time. The gap initiates a strong downtrend later.

## How to trade gaps using supply and demand

To make the best use of gaps in trading, we must first determine whether the gap is a starting or an ending gap.

A starting gap indicates a continuation of the (new) trend initiated by the gap, whereas an ending gap shows a potential reversal of the trend.

In terms of supply and demand trading, a starting gap provides an initial signal of a new trend. Traders will need to pay more attention to the *price zone* just before the gap for a potential price test. On the contrary, an ending gap normally signals a potential end of the prevailing trend.

### Ending gaps

*Principle:* You look for a supply or demand zone corresponding to the gap. This is where you can place an entry.

Take the chart below as an example.

101

On this chart, we have a gap up after a long uptrend. The first thing we do is to look back to history to see whether there is any supply zone created at a similar level of the gap. Once you've identified and drawn the zone successfully, you can place a short position using a market order or a limit order.

A market order is suitable if the gap violates the supply zone immediately. If the gap is just about to touch the opposing zone, you can consider placing a limit order (a sell order in the example above) and waiting for the order to be triggered.

The sample principle also applies in the example below where a gap pierces a supply zone formed previously, initiating a new downtrend.

102

GBP/USD
Daily chart

Supply zone

Ending gap

**Principle:** There are three steps of trading with starting gaps:

- We start by using the gap to draw the supply or demand zone (this is the zone before the gap occurrence, not the other way round);
- Place a limit order at the newly drawn zone;
- Wait for the price to come back to the zone for the order to be absorbed.

Basically, a starting gap appears right after the end of a trend and it may trigger a new market imbalance. This is why it is connected with reversal trading.

Let's look at the example below.

On this chart, a starting gap up appeared after a long downtrend. We use the gap to draw a demand zone at the bottom of the chart and place a buy limit entry along the way. Soon after the gap was formed, the price came back quickly to this newly created zone before making a nice rally. In this case, a gap is an early signal of a trend reversal.

Let's move to another example.

In this example, we have a sustained uptrend in place before two consecutive gaps down appeared in the opposite direction of the trend. To trade this starting gap, we base on the candlestick just before the gap occurrence to draw a supply zone and place a sell limit order. The price quickly jumped back up to test the zone before going all the way down.

Now, let's remember the first odd enhancer in trading with supply and demand and you would understand more about the importance of gaps: *how the price leaves the zone*.

Notice in the example above, the supply zone is just above the gap. A prompt bounce from the zone means that the price left the zone strongly and decisively, signaling a great imbalance of the market, and there is a high possibility of the price going in the new direction of the trend. Considering this, trading reversal with starting gaps is often a safe and effective option to adopt.

To many traders, gaps are a gold mine in trading. If you understand the mechanics behind each gap and confidently identify the type of gap on a chart (starting or ending), you stand a good chance of grasping the best opportunities to stack some good profits.

105

While executing trades with gaps individually may create some confusion among traders, combining them with supply and demand zones can make things clearer and easier. In some cases, gaps could play as high-level confirmation signals that enhance the probability of trade success.

In the next chapter, we'll learn the first technical indicator in conjunction with supply and demand zones.

# Chapter 11: CCI Techniques

While I rarely treat technical indicators as the core of my trading system, I still use them as confirmation signals in many cases. By adding technical indicators to our trading arsenal, we can better filter out false signals in unpredictable financial markets. As long as we use indicators for confirmation purposes only, trading with them will be less stressful while enhancing your winning probability.

In this chapter, we'll learn about an indicator called "CCI", what it tells us, and how to execute supply and demand trading more flexibly and effectively with the help of the CCI indicator.

## What is CCI?

CCI is the abbreviation of the Commodity Channel Index, measuring the price momentum in the market. Among the most popular functions in the CCI is determining overbought/oversold areas and the health of the trend on the chart. In this chapter, we'll focus more on the latter in combination with supply and demand trading.

As always, CCI is best used with the help of multiple timeframe analyses. The longer frames will be used to determine the overall trend of the market while the shorter ones will be more suitable for spotting minor retracements for entry purposes.

## CCI Readings

The CCI oscillator moves up and down all the time, with the zero (0) level the middle line. Observing the CCI gives us an idea of the historical averages of an asset. When the CCI indicator is located below the zero level, the price is lower than the historical average. Otherwise, it is above the historical average. Take a look at the example below:

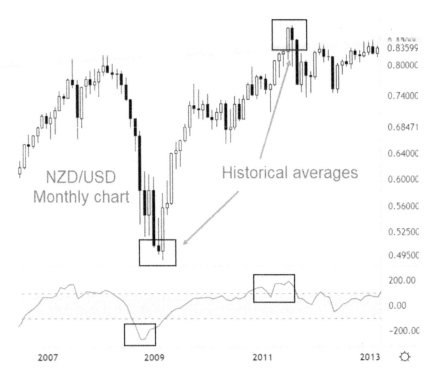

NZD/USD
Monthly chart

Historical averages

On this chart, the price formed a new swing high or a new swing low when the corresponding CCI indicator reading is above the 100 level or below the -100 level.

Another useful function of a CCI indicator is identifying the market's trend. When the oscillator crosses above the zero level to the +100 level, the market is likely to be in an uptrend. Whereas, if the price cross below the zero level to the -100 level, the corresponding price is likely to be in a downtrend. While this is not always the case, it could be referred to after other price action methods have been taken into account.

Like some other lagging indicators, there are cases when the indicator hovers around the +100 or -100 level longer than expected. This may result from an extended uptrend or downtrend where the buyers or sellers are dominating the market without losing momentum over the short term.

Now that we've had some understanding of the CCI oscillator, let's move to the main part of this chapter: how to combine CCI with supply and demand trading.

## Trade supply and demand using CCI

Principle:

In a downtrend, we only consider shorting when the price is above the 100 level. We look for signs of gradual weakness from the dominating player before identifying an entry level.

In an uptrend, we only consider going long if the price is below the -100 level. We watch out for signals of lost momentum from the dominating player before choosing an entry price.

In both cases, we can use the 20-day moving average for more confirmation of the trend. In an uptrend, we remain our long position if the price is well above the 20-day moving average, whereas the price remaining below the 20-moving average could be a positive signal of a sustained downtrend.

Take a look at the two examples below:

Using the CCI, we can partly explain how certain price actions or zones fail to work in some cases. Let's take the chart below as an example.

On this chart, a demand zone was created within the trend (a rally-base-rally pattern). While this pattern is generally not an ideal environment for the reversal to happen, let's discover some other reasons why the zone failed to work in this case.

First, it's not fresh. Right after the formation of the zone, the price tested it and bounced back to the upside drastically for a long period before visiting the zone for the second time. In other words, this zone is not optimized in terms of freshness.

Second, by drawing a trend line, we can see the price broke the trend line and went all the way down. A sustained uptrend was threatened.

Third, notice how the price quickly created an opposing supply zone after the second visit to the zone, not to mention the fact that the price left the zone in a weak fashion with multiple indecision candlesticks. This tells us that another strong uptrend may be hard to achieve, and the downtrend may continue over the short term.

What we could do is to wait for other price actions and consider a short position when we have a confluence between the CCI and the supply/demand zone.

Because we've had a previous supply zone, we wait for the price to come back to this zone with a confirmation from the CCI reading – which is around the 200 level at the time of the test. Notice how strongly and decisively the price left the zone when it was created, making it a potential trade area for the short advocate.

All these conditions have paved the way for us to open a market order at the newly formed supply zone.

Here is another example.

In this example, an uptrend was in place and a trend line was drawn to confirm the bullish market trend. On the other hand, we draw two demand zones to place limit orders. Notice how the demand zones and the trend lines together form a confluence effect, giving us two good opportunities to enter high probability trades.

Moreover, we receive green-light signals from the CCI oscillator. Notice how the corresponding readings are below the -100 level each time the price visited the demand zone. Even if we fail, we can tell ourselves we've tried our best to optimize the trade, and there may not be so much regret or depression. One thing I can ensure: if you always stick to trade optimization, you'll stand a good chance of having sustainable success.

### Managing positions with CCI indicator

There are two ways we can use the CCI oscillator to manage our positions: add or close our trading positions.

Principle:

If the oscillator's reading is retracing back down below the +100 level (in an uptrend) or above the -100 level (in a downtrend), we consider a full or partial exit. When the reading is towards the zero line, it can either be a price correction or reversal. In any case, we only add in another position if the reading is above the zero line in an uptrend, or below the zero line in a downtrend.

In the example above, the price made a strong uptrend before a slight correction happened. We look for the CCI reading to cross above the zero line again for another buy entry.

Using the CCI indicator effectively entails a lot of practice and a great combination with other trading tools. Instead of relying wholly on it as a trade signal, we should use CCI to get a better view of the predominant trend in the market. Other than that, using the CCI indicator as a trade alert when it hovers around the oversold and overbought levels enables us to make the most out of the price swing in the market.

# Chapter 12: Multi-Frame Analysis 101

Even you employ the best trading strategies and make sure that all odd enhancers are satisfied, you may put your trades in danger if you fail to apply multiple frame (MTF) analysis in trading. From my observation, ignoring MTF analysis is the No.1 reason for losses in trading with supply and demand.

Multiple timeframe analysis is widely used by most professional traders. MTF allows traders and investors to grasp the big picture of the market and remove dangerous market noise.

In this chapter, we'll start by learning about different trading styles and determining which timeframes go with each trading style in MTF analysis. Then, we'll go into the core of MTF trading: *the curve and smaller zone within it*. Each of these zones contains a different message and understanding which phase we are in shapes the way we analyze the next price movements. The main goal in exploring smaller curves is to make sure we go with the trend, not against it. We want to buy low and sell high, not the other way round.

### What is multiple timeframe analysis?

Basically, multiple timeframe analysis is the process of analyzing your assets/instruments in more than one timeframe to get a better understanding of how it is performing in the market.

Our goal is to reach an alignment in the signals cultivated from all the timeframes we choose. Normally, we'll give the signals on longer timeframes a priority. If what the lower frames tell is different from the bigger frame's signal, we wait until all the frames have reached an alignment.

There is no fixed recommended timeframe for traders to choose in trading because not all traders share the same trading style. In general, you will start by defining which type of trader you are, then select the timeframes to analyze your asset price. I recommend from two to three timeframes (ideally three) to grasp a good understanding of the price direction.

## Trading styles

There are four different trading styles mainly based on the length of the trade and your tolerance degree. If you want to make some quick bucks within a few minutes, you are a scalper. If you are more patient and remain in a trade position for a few days or even weeks, you are a swing trader.

Four trading styles include:

- Scalping,
- Day Trading,
- Swing Trading,
- Position Trading.

You may hear about them here and there, but we still recap some main points about them.

### Scalping

A trader who enjoys scalping is called a scalper. A scalper's goal is to profit from the smallest price fluctuations in the market. It means that he/she must spend most of his/her time in front of the trading screens. A scalper may execute from 10 to 30 trades per day on average.

Scalping entails good risk management skills. Trading with small timeframes means you're in and out of the trades quite frequently within the day. A failure to manage what you are doing could lead to an accumulated loss and take your account to dangers.

Also, because you take many trades, remember to take the broker's fees into account. It may seem trivial at first, but gradually these fees add up and exert a considerable impact on your equity.

Another aspect to consider is the amount of stress you may endure when seeing a lot of price fluctuations throughout the day, especially if many of them don't align with your expectation.

### Day trading

Similar to scalpers, day traders open and close their trades within the day. However, traders hold their trades much longer instead of exiting within minutes. And because of this, a day trader often takes much fewer trades compared to scalpers (less than 10 trades).

## Swing trading

This style is preferred by many traders because it requires less time in front of the trading screen and removes unnecessary stress due to price fluctuations. They tend to hold their trades as long as the medium-trend is valid. Being a swing trader entails greater patience than a typical day trader.

Generally, a swing trade can last from a few days to multiple weeks, depending on market conditions.

## Position trading

The last type in the list is position trading, where traders hold their trades for a long time, i.e from a few months to a few years.

Understandably, position traders are those who are extremely patient and have the nerves of steel and often own large trading capital. They use not only technical analysis but also fundamental analysis where they take several economic factors into consideration.

## **Timeframe combination**

Now that we've understood some characteristics of each trading style, let's define the best timeframe combination for each type of trading. Ideally, three timeframes are recommended for the best combination.

A scalper can use a combination of 15-minute, 5-minute, and 1-minute charts to read market fluctuations. Among these ones, the 15-minute chart is the longer/bigger timeframe, the 5-minute chart is the medium timeframe, and the 1-minute chart is the shorter timeframe.

In day trading, we use the daily chart as the longer frame, the 4-hour chart as the medium frame, and the 1-hour chart as the shorter timeframe for analysis.

A swing trader will focus on the weekly, daily, and 4-hour charts respectively to analyze market conditions.

A position trader will focus on the three longest timeframes. The monthly, weekly, and daily charts would be the longer, medium, and shorter timeframes respectively.

There is no right or wrong in choosing two, three, or four different timeframes. A combination of three frames is based on my personal experience, which enhances your trading performance and avoids making it so complicated. In some simple chart conditions, two frames might be enough for effective chart analysis.

### How to determine supply and demand curve

After you've identified your trading style and the time frames you'll use for analysis, it's time to start working with the curve. A curve is simply the area between the two proximal lines of the nearest demand zone and supply zone in control. Trading with MTF entails working on the curve in a longer timeframe. Using the curve as the core of MTF trading, everything would be clear and simple. Let's get into it.

1. Identify the longer timeframe to use

We always start with the longest frame in the trio, also called the longer/bigger timeframe (in comparison with the two remaining ones).

2. Identify the nearest supply and demand

After switching our chart to the longer timeframe, we identify the two nearest supply and demand zones to the current price level.

Looking at the monthly chart below, we have one supply zone and one demand zone, and the current price is closer to the demand zone.

3. Splitting the curve

As I mentioned from the beginning of the chapter, when we split the big zone (the area between two proximal lines) into smaller zones, we have different potential zones for trade entry purposes.

In this step, we divide the said big zone into three equal ones. The area used for such division is bound by two proximal lines. After the division, we have three small zones, namely High, Equilibrium, and Low. These areas are illustrated in the picture below.

As you can see from the chart, we have five total areas on the chart. The supply zone is considered very high in the curve while the demand zone is very low in the curve. The current price is located in the equilibrium price area.

There are two options to split the big zone. First, you based on the price margin between the two proximal lines, then divide the margin by three different parts.

For example, if the two proximal lines are located at $10 and $13 respectively, then each smaller zone is $1 wide (= (13-10)/3). By drawing two horizontal

120

lines at 11 and 12, we now have three different smaller zones: high, equilibrium, and low.

Another option in drawing these lines is to use the Fibonacci retracement tool, which is familiar to most traders. There are some default set levels in the Fibonacci retracement tools which are derived from the magical mathematical Fibonacci sequence back in the 13th century. However, this tool can be used to plot *any desired levels* we need between a swing high and a swing low.

In this case, we aim at dividing the curve into three smaller ones, hence we set one level at the 33% value and another level at the 66% value as shown in the picture below.

After the customization step, we now have three equal zones: high, equilibrium, and low. Now, let's explore what we will do with these smaller zones.

121

## Trading with the curve

On the longer timeframe, we look at the curve and determine whether the current price is in the upper part, lower part, or in the middle of the curve. Based on this information, we decide which position we are in over the next market moves.

- When the price is from **high** to **very high** in the curve, we sell only.
- When the price is from **low** to **very low** in the curve, we buy only.
- When the price is in the **equilibrium zone**, we can choose to trade with the predominant trend or avoid trading.

Now that we've been equipped with everything for a trade, let's put them together to define a trade entry using supply and demand theories.

In the example below, we start from the monthly chart. First, we determine the current price level and the two nearest supply and demand zone. After that, we determine smaller zones using the Fibonacci retracement tool.

The current price is positioned at the border between an equilibrium zone and the low zone, thus we can expect a long entry as long as the trend remains bullish.

Now, let's see what happened in the weekly chart.

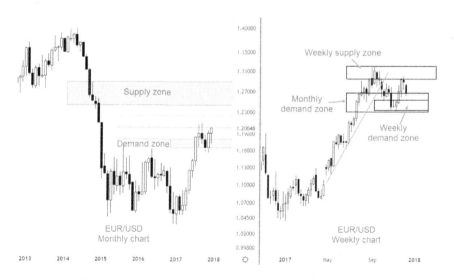

123

On the weekly chart, the price created a supply zone before breaking the trend line. It continued to fall before creating a demand zone that is overlapped with the monthly zone.

Selling at the weekly demand zone can be dangerous because you are going against the primary trend (monthly uptrend). The longer frame always wins, hence we should pay respect to its signal. Hence, we avoid a short position in this case. Instead, we wait for the price to go back down to the monthly/weekly demand zone for a long position.

On this chart, we can see the price visited the demand zone before surging. As long as we trade in the direction signal of the longer frame, we're safe with our decision. At this level, buyers are more interested in initiating or adding more positions. Understanding which phase/trade zone we are in helps to avoid giving our hard-earned money to the market.

Let's move to another example where we use three timeframes instead of two.

In this example, the price is high on the curve, hence we only look for a short position, ideally with a fresh zone in a shorter timeframe. Below is the weekly chart of the same currency pair.

On the weekly chart, it is clear that an uptrend was in place where higher highs and higher lows were formed. We draw demand and supply zones to predict whether there are high probability zones or not. In this case, the weekly supply and demand zones in control are overlapped with the monthly zones, meaning that they are potential zones to trade. Yet, since the price is high on the curve, we only consider the supply zone at the top of the chart for a limit order.

You can consider a limit order right at the proximal line of the weekly supply zone in this case. The price is near a very potential price zone drawn on a weekly chart. Things are in favor of a sell limit order. One important thing we should take into consideration is the stop-loss: is it too far from the entry price? If the stop range is bigger than our tolerance limit, you should switch to a shorter timeframe. Given that, let's look at the daily chart.

On the daily chart, we have a supply area nested inside both the weekly and monthly zones, which is perfect in terms of zone confluence. We place a sell limit order at the proximal line with the stop loss just above the distal line (using the daily chart, we now have a smaller stop). The risk/reward ratio is around 1:3 – ideal for a trade. The exit price would be at the demand zone's proximal line.

Below is what happened later.

Daily supply zone    Entry    Risk

Weekly proximal line

Monthly proximal line

Targeted

EUR/USD
Daily chart

1.50000
1.48000
1.46000
1.44000
1.42000
1.40997
1.40000
1.38000
1.36000
1.34000
1.32000
1.30200
1.28400

Feb    Mar    Apr    May    Jun

The price hit the limit price and went all the way down to the target very quickly, indicating how strong the supply zone is.

Also, you can see how placing a trade in a shorter timeframe could be a much wiser decision. If you choose the monthly proximal line, you can be more nervous when the price pierced more than half of the monthly supply zone. On the other hand, if you choose the daily chart for an entry level, the price touched the proximal line slightly before quickly reversing to the downside.

MTF analysis may be complicated at first. There are tons of market conditions, and it isn't easy to spot a perfect alignment among all three timeframes most of the time. Often, traders need to wait, but it's worth your time.

MTF analysis entails identifying the curve and analyzing the current price position correctly to avoid going against the trend. Once you've mastered these things, trading will become much simpler. Bear in mind the longer timeframe always wins. Sadly, few traders pay attention to this. Multiple timeframe analysis may not produce a lot of trade signals. Instead, it serves to filter higher-probability signals only.

Trading is not about how many trades you place, but how much you make from the trades you place.

# Chapter 13: Trade Examples

In this chapter, we'll learn how to trade using supply and demand theory in the combination of other tools and methods. We'll act as a long-term trader and analyze a currency chart via different timeframes.

## Selecting a larger timeframe

First, we select a larger timeframe to identify the two nearest supply and demand zones, as well as determine whether the current price is high or low in the curve.

The monthly timeframe is selected because we act as a position trader.

From the chart, we can see the price is approaching the monthly demand zone, which is between the 1.38925 – 1.47408 range. Without having to split the curve into smaller areas, it is clear that the price is *low in the curve*. This means that we consider a buy order only. Yet, considering a large zone range in the monthly chart, we never place an entry and stop-loss order using this chart.

Now, let's move to the weekly chart to see what happened:

## A deeper look into the trend

On the weekly chart, the price was in a downtrend with consecutive lower highs and lower lows.

The price is testing the 1.47408 price level for a second time. As you remember, this is the proximal line of the monthly demand zone.

But the nearest weekly demand zone is a little lower, between the 1.38989 - 1.43107 price range. This means that the weekly demand zone is nested inside the monthly ones, making it a potential area for an entry.

Looking at the zones above, we have two supply zones formed as a result of continuation patterns at the 1.58497-1.60822 and 1.64365-1.67244 ranges. Located at the top of the chart is a strong supply zone in the 1.72669-1.78870 range, which is overlapped with the monthly one.

## Be prepared for an imminent trade

On the daily chart, we look for a fresh demand zone to place our trade. Remember we only consider a buy entry in this case.

On this chart, we have a demand zone between the 1.41557 and 1.44104 price levels (zone 1), which is nested inside the weekly and monthly demand zones. If the price can retrace back down to this zone, this would be perfect. However, we should be in a position to buy as soon as the price approaches the monthly proximal level instead of waiting for it to touch the daily proximal one. More on that in the next section.

Notice by switching to the daily chart, we have narrowed the demand range – or reduced the distance between the entry price (the proximal line) and the stop price (just below the distal line).

Regarding the supply zone, there is one that is spotted between the 1.62182 and the 1.63439 level (zone 2). Interestingly, this zone is nested inside the weekly zone.

Now that we've identified a lot of potential trade areas across different timeframes, let's move to the most important part: how to enter and manage your positions.

## How to trade

Let's look deeper into the daily chart. As we can see, the price hovered around the monthly proximal line for some time but failed to extend to the expected daily demand zone. As I said before, we shouldn't pay all attention to the pre-defined daily zone, but watch closely at daily price actions when it starts violating a big zone – the monthly area.

Given that, we find a daily demand zone at the 1.45322-1.46818 range (the "new zone"), which also coincides with the monthly one.

The price revisited the demand zone and broke above the trend line as indicated in the chart above. The potential profit target on the daily chart should be the 1.62182 price level, which is a fresh and confluence zone. Let's see what happened next:

The price broke the trend line, forming another demand zone on its way to the target. This is the zone traders can consider adding other positions. As long as the trend is confirmed on the larger timeframe and the price doesn't violate a selling area (high or very high in the curve), entering another trade (even with a less ideal price) would not be a bad idea. The chart below showed what happened next once another trade is triggered at the newly formed demand zone.

On this chart, the price had some difficulties at the newly formed demand zone, but finally, it managed to surge to the monthly supply area. We've moved a long way since the entry price level, hence it's better we lock in part of the profit at this area and let the remaining part run to see if it can reach our final target. As can be seen from the chart below, it didn't take long for the price to reach the 1.62182 target.

Things may not stop here because a price retracement may serve to form another fresh supply zone.

On this chart, as soon as the price broke the ascending trend line to the downside, it created a new supply zone right at the breaking level, between the 1.58931-1.60123 range.

Notice the price has not violated a sell zone on the monthly chart, we should still be in a position for a buy trade. The best way to do this is by looking at a confluence area between the daily and weekly charts.

In this case, a buy limit order is placed around the 1.53568 level (the proximal border) of the daily zone nested inside the weekly zone.

As can be seen in the chart below, the price fell sharply to this expected demand zone before making a strong rally up.

This example teaches us about the importance of following the predominant trend in the market as well as how to manage the trade to make the most out of a strong move. As a trader, you should always monitor in which part of the big curve the price is to prepare for the next strategies and techniques. As long as the price hasn't violated the selling zones (high or very high in the curve), we can be confident in following a bullish trend. On the contrary, once the price hasn't violated buying areas (low or very low in the curve), we can consider a sell order.

# Chapter 14: Risk Management In Trading

Any professional trader in the world understands the role of risk management in their trading process. Applying effective risk management strategies, traders are able to control their trades, minimize unnecessary losses, and make consistent profits.

As you may already hear, trading is not being right or wrong in any individual trade, it's about how much you make when you're right and how much you lose when you're wrong. This emphasizes the importance of trade management and reminds us to focus on quality instead of the quantity of the trade.

In this chapter, we'll go over a few components of risk management in trading that you must pay relentless attention to.

## What is risk management?

There are a lot of ways to define *"risk management"*. To me, risk management in trading is a method of managing your losses so that they won't go beyond your tolerance. In other words, risk management is the art of keeping your trading under control.

The underlying reason for risk management is simple: any trader in the world encounters losing trades again and again in their trading career (as a result of unpredictable market movements), hence unless you manage your trades well, you won't survive in this endeavor long.

Traders can't control where the market will go, but they **can** control and ensure their trading rules are complied with: when to trade, when to stand on the sidelines, the risked amount, the number of trades, and so on. When you stick to complying with all components in risk management, you remove a lot of negative psychological factors that can ruin your account.

## Avoid a margin call

Simply put, a margin call happens when your trading equity is below the minimum required amount for your trades to be taken. In this case, there will a message from the broker to make an additional deposit so that you will be able to take the next trades. With this deposit, you are able to cover the unexpected loss(es) that may incur during your trade process.

Based on the extent of risk exposure you take and the leverage you use, a margin call can be determined.

For example: if you choose a leverage 0f x10 and you lose 10% of your account, you'll get a margin call. If you choose a leverage of x5 and you lose 20% of your account, a margin call will occur.

Suppose you choose to deposit an amount of $1,000 and a leverage of 100:1. This means that your risk exposure is $100,000. If you lose 1% of your exposure amount ($1,000), you'll get a margin call.


## How much to risk?

As a rule of thumb, you shouldn't risk more than 2% in any individual trade. And this 2% threshold is for experienced traders only. If you are a newbie trader, stick to 1% until you are successful with your trades (i.e tripling your trading equity) before thinking of increasing your risk exposure.

In trading, risk management will boil down to where you put your stop loss and how many units of assets you will buy or sell. Without stop-loss, you can't implement any risk management strategies.

For example, you choose a risk exposure of 2% for each trade. Let's say your account equity is $10,000, hence for every trade you take, you'll not risk more than $200.

Abiding by the 2% rule helps you stay within a safe parameter to prevent things from going out of control.

Let's switch to the comparison table below to understand that just a small adjustment of the risk exposure can have a great impact on our account balance.

In this table, two traders share the same initial capital amount of $1,000. However, the first trader chooses a 2% risk exposure while the second one adopts the 5% risk exposure. If both of them have 1o losing trades in a row, the first one still has $833,79 left, while the second one only has $630.25 in their account.

| Trades | Account balance | 2% Risk Per Trade | Account balance | 5% Risk Per Trade |
|--------|-----------------|-------------------|-----------------|-------------------|
| 1 | 1,000.00 | 20.00 | 1,000.00 | 50.00 |
| 2 | 980.00 | 19.60 | 950.00 | 47.50 |
| 3 | 960.40 | 19.21 | 902.50 | 45.13 |
| 4 | 941.19 | 18.82 | 857.38 | 42.87 |
| 5 | 922.37 | 18.45 | 814.51 | 40.73 |
| 6 | 903.92 | 18.08 | 773.78 | 38.69 |
| 7 | 885.84 | 17.72 | 735.09 | 36.75 |
| 8 | 868.13 | 17.36 | 698.34 | 34.92 |
| 9 | 850.76 | 17.02 | 663.42 | 33.17 |
| 10 | 833.75 | 16.67 | 630.25 | 31.51 |

By being patient and sticking to the rule of risk exposure, we would feel much more relaxed and comfortable in taking trades.

## How to calculate position size

Position sizing is a technique that determines how many units of assets you will buy so that your loss will not surpass your risk exposure in case the stop-loss is hit.

Position size = Risk amount/difference between entry and stop price

For example, you have a $1,000 trading account and choose a 2% risk level that is $20. You buy a stock at the price of $10, with the stop-loss at $8. The size of your position will be 20/(10-8) = 10. You will buy 10 stocks.

If you are a forex trader, things are a little complicated but don't worry, everything will be as easy as pie. Let's discover.

In trading currency pairs, the risk is calculated in the quote currency. For example, if you trade AUD/USD, the quote currency is USD. If you trade USD/CAD, the quote currency is CAD.

Let's take two scenarios as examples:

Suppose you have a $100,000 account. Using the 2% rule, you risk $2000 in each trade.

1.   If you want to go long on AUD/USD:

Entry price: 0.6900

Stop-loss: 0.6200 (700 pips)

Quote currency: USD

Risk: $200

Position size: = 200/700 = 0.29 mini lot = 0.029 standard lot.

In this case, if your stop-loss is hit, you will lose $200. Note that there might be commission fees or overnight fees/gain depending on the length of your position.


2.   If you want to go short on USD/JPY:

Entry price: 119.00

Stop-loss: 124.00 (500 pips)

Quote currency: JPY

Risk: 200*119.00 = 23,800 JPY

Pip Value: 23,800/500 = 47.6 JPY

Position size: 4.76 micro lots or 0.0476 standard lot.


## The threat from the drawdown

Few people pay attention to drawdown, but saying no to trading based on a specific drawdown level prevents things from getting out of control, and helps you regain a more balanced state of mind.

Basically, a drawdown is a difference between the high and the low of your account balance. Say you deposit $10,000 into your trading account. After a period, your account balance drops to $7,000, causing a $3,000 drawdown (=$10,000 - $7,000).

Personally, I set my drawdown level at 20%. This means that for any reason I've lost 20% from the peak of my account balance, I'll stay away from the trading screen for the rest of the month.

Also, when experiencing a drawdown, I will lower my risk exposure by 25%, for example from 2% to 1.5%. I will not restore my risk exposure until my account regains its previous high.

From my experience, managing risks in the financial market is not a complicated task, but a difficult one. The biggest obstacle in managing your trades doesn't have anything to do with the markets, but yourself. You have to cope with the temptation to increase your risk exposure and position sizes all the time. Also, you will need to resist the temptation of adding more trades when you're making losses because those are the times you are the most fragile and vulnerable to market and psychological traps.

Managing your trade is, to some extent, a tedious task. But it's worth it because it saves you in the long run. Be calm, start loving risk management more, and see big positive impacts.

# Conclusion

We've gone over nearly everything you'll need to trade successfully with supply and demand in the financial markets. The biggest advantage in using supply and demand is you can jump on the same board with big players in the market. This alone might be enough for you to consider using these theories frequently in your trading career, not to mention a number of advantages that supply and demand trading has over traditional support and resistance levels.

Some people attribute supply and demand trading to set-and-forget trading where traders just wait for the price to trigger the limit order, and done. I tend to disagree. Being a supply and demand trader, you should be flexible in trading with the zones. Not all zones are tested as we expect. Some will work, some won't. The art of catching a great price test lies in the ability to determine potential zones on a lower timeframe other than the ones you've identified on larger frames.

One of the best components in trading with supply and demand zones is the scoring system, which helps you less vulnerable to emotional and arbitrary trading. Sticking to a score measurement table enables you to better comply with your trading rules, which often seem too vague to most traders. By applying the scoring system for a long enough period of time, you'll see how effective it is to prevent you from taking unadvisable trades. You'll see that you've taken fewer trades, but the winning rate is obviously higher.

One last thing: risk management. It's never redundant to talk about this topic because poor trade management is the number one reason for account blow-ups in trading. While the scoring system enables you to optimize your trade entry and exit prices, good risk management strategies help to put your account in good control and never let losses run beyond your tolerance. Good trading means good account management. Simple as that.

So, we've come near the end of this book. If you're reading this section, I would like to congratulate you because I firmly believe what you've learned in this book is well worth your time and will pay off in the long run.

I suggest you back-test as many candlestick charts as possible on the superb Tradingview platform that comes in the material that you've downloaded in the middle of the book. I really hope you can grasp the shared supply and demand strategies because I believe they all benefit you both in short-term and long-term trading.

Finally, if you feel you've learned something useful in this book, please consider leaving an honest review. I would be very, very grateful to you.

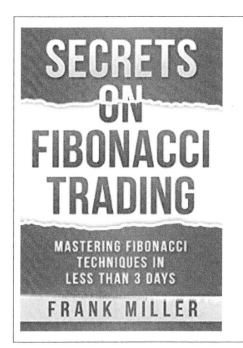

Scan this barcode with your phone camera to check out my No.1 book on Fibonacci trading.

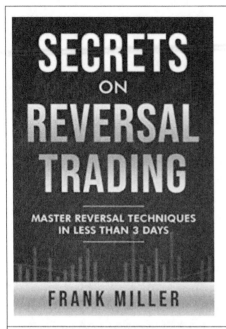

Scan this barcode with your phone camera to check out my No.1 book on reversal trading techniques.

Scan this barcode with your phone camera to check out a professionally designed trading journal and master discipline in trading.

# CRYPTO MASTER

## THE ULTIMATE BEGINNER'S GUIDE TO CRYPTOCURRENCY TRADING AND INVESTING

### FRANK MILLER

Scan this barcode with your phone camera to get everything you need to profit from crypto trading and investing.

(A perfect summary of my 7-year journey with cryptocurrency market).

# References:

(2021, November 11). Supply and Demand Forex – The Highest Accuracy Method. The5ers.

https://the5ers.com/supply-and-demand-forex/

What is Supply and Demand in Forex? Tradingfxhub.

https://tradingfxhub.com/blog/what-is-supply-and-demand-in-forex/

The Ultimate Guide to Master Supply and Demand in Forex. Tradingfxhub.

https://tradingfxhub.com/blog/the-ultimate-guide-to-master-supply-and-demand-in-forex/

*How to Identify Supply and Demand Zones?* Tradingfxhub.

https://tradingfxhub.com/blog/how-to-identify-supply-and-demand-zones-in-forex/

The Difference Between Fresh and Original Levels. Tradingfxhub.

https://tradingfxhub.com/blog/the-difference-between-fresh-and-original-levels/

How to Score Supply and Demand Zones? Tradingfxhub.

https://tradingfxhub.com/blog/how-to-score-supply-and-demand-zones/

Multiple Time Frame Analysis in Forex. Tradingfxhub.

https://tradingfxhub.com/blog/multiple-time-frame-analysis-in-forex/

How to Trade Supply and Demand with Price Action. Tradingfxhub.

https://tradingfxhub.com/blog/how-to-trade-supply-and-demand-with-price-action/

How to Identify and Trade a Flip Zone in Forex. Tradingfxhub.

https://tradingfxhub.com/blog/how-to-identify-and-trade-a-flip-zone-in-forex/

How to Trade Supply and Demand Patterns [Reversal & Continuation Patterns]. Tradingfxhub.

https://tradingfxhub.com/blog/how-to-trade-supply-and-demand-patterns-reversal-continuation-patterns/

How to Trade Gaps using Supply and Demand. Tradingfxhub.

https://tradingfxhub.com/blog/how-to-trade-gaps-using-supply-and-demand/

How to Trade Supply and Demand using CCI. Tradingfxhub.

https://tradingfxhub.com/blog/how-to-trade-supply-and-demand-using-cci/

How to Identify Supply and Demand Curve? Tradingfxhub.

https://tradingfxhub.com/blog/how-to-identify-supply-and-demand-curve/

Risk Management Guide for Forex Traders. Tradingfxhub.

https://tradingfxhub.com/blog/risk-management-guide-for-forex-traders/